My Unicorn Has Gone Away

*Life, Death, Grief and Living
In the Years of AIDS*

Robert J. L. Publicover

My Unicorn Has Gone Away

Life, Death, Grief and Living
In the Years of AIDS

Robert J. L. Publicover

Powder House Publishing
P.O. Box 137
Somerville, MA 02144
(617) 666-1848

*All profits from this book go to the
Committee For A Response To AIDS*

ISBN 0-9634759-0-8
Library of Congress Catalog Number 92-062037

Second Edition 1993 Powder House Publishing

Printed in the United States of America

Additional copies available from:
   Powder House Publishing
   P.O. Box 137
   Somerville, MA 02144
   (617) 666-1848

Dedicated to
JOHN HEDLEY CARABINERIS, JR.
and to all of those who have
lost a loved one

Happy are those who dream dreams
and are ready to pay the price
to make them come true.

— L. J. Cardinal Svenens

Contents

Contents, cont.

Robert J.L. Publicover, John H. Carabineris, Jr., T. Michael Markowski

I Cried

I cried today.
I cried as I watch a fine young man that I love
  Lie nearly comatose in his hospital room.
I cried for our love.
I cried for his youth.
I cried because I'm selfish and don't want to lose him.
I cried for his parents who care so much.
I cried for the thousands who have already gone.
I cried for the millions who will die from this plague.
I cried for the others who care so much about him.
I cried because his only worry is that he will be a burden.
I cried for the President, who still does not understand
  That there is a plague in our land.
I cried because I know that my day will come.
I cried as I understood how much his nurses care about him.
I cried for his doctor, who must watch so many leave him.
I cried for the dozens and dozens of people who care
  They send so many cards and flowers.
I cried more for the man who said he would not.
I cried for Michael, Tim, Lois, Larry, who love him, too.
I cried for the friends who have been so supportive of us.
  And then I stopped crying
  So that I can be strong for him.

Bluntly Speaking: Do It Now!
(The Somerville News, March 4, 1992)

I've written before about Friendship. I've written about telling your friends, your lovers, and other people whom you care about how you feel. I've written about doing things today because you never know when tomorrow won't be there.

My parents never fully could understand that theory, nor can many people that I talk to from their generation. Oh, yes, I truly believe in the work ethic, but I also firmly believe in taking the time out to smell the roses.

In January, we were having tough weeks at the Somerville News. There were not many ads coming in, thanks to the recession which George Bush still doesn't understand. Finances were getting tougher, with a tenant who had not paid rent for 8 months. Christmas had not been quite as good as in past years. My partner, John Carabineris, complained because his own finances were so bad that he could not do what he wanted to for his family and friends. It had put a damper on his holiday.

On Tuesday morning, I walked into the office and told John to close his roll top desk and go home and pack an overnight bag. I headed over to Baker Travel and picked up Amtrak tickets to New York City.

At this point I should note that this story begins back in November. Way back when, I had really gone off the deep end and ordered two $100 tickets to see "Miss Saigon" on Broadway. One of them was John's Christmas present. We headed off in the old "My News" mobile. Thanks to my Highland Avenue mechanic, who assured me that there was nothing wrong with my thermostat, we decided to drive. We got about 60 miles before the car overheated and we barely made it back, cracking a head gasket in the process. No show, no $100 seats... and you wonder why Christmas was a downer?

So...I, we, packed that overnight bag and headed off to NYC on the train, after a cup of cappucino at South Station. We stayed at the magnificent new Marriott Marquis in the middle of Times Square. The first night I got tickets to "The Secret Garden"—somehow, we got 5th row tickets. The play was OK. The next day I stood in line at the 1/2 price ticket booth and got 4th row seats to "City of Angels." It was an enjoyable play, which we did not realize was closing that Sunday.

Before we went to see "City of Angels," we decided to check out the revolving restaurant at the Marriott. We thought it was on the 4th floor, but that turned out to be the revolving bar. Instead, we found a long ramp which led only to a maitre d' and an elevator. We had no reservations.About half way up the winding ramp, sat one of those elegant plastic holders with the menu...and prices.

Whew. We stood and looked at the prices and I think John said something like "we shouldn't do that." After a few seconds more of contemplation, we started back down the ramp, perhaps to head back to HoJo's. John was just ahead of me. I do not know why, but I stopped dead in my tracks and called him back.

I remember my words very well. "We only go this way once, c'mon." We walked back up the ramp. The restaurant turned out to be on the 48th floor. We had superb appetizers and a wonderful meal as we revolved, watching New York City far below.

The next day we headed home on Amtrak. We ran into a couple of friends whom we talked with for much of the trip. We had a great time.

John came down with a 103° fever a few days later. He's been in the hospital quite a while now, and it looks like we won't be going to New York City again.

Don't wait to do those special things.

Oh, God, how I love this man

Oh, God, how I love this man.

A simple statement it would seem. It is not. I look back now at the times we had and I have a terrible sense of guilt that I could never be happy with him, that I always found the faults and never the good things...that I loved him best when he ran off to P'town or Phoenix or now that he is soon to leave me.

We did not have a terrible life but it would have been so much better if I had only realized what I had. I wonder if many other couples have the same problem. People tell me how much he loves me and I know they are right. Without thinking of it, he must have forgiven me so many times for the way I treated him. Sometimes he got so bitter when we argued but we always got over it. I felt that we got over it too fast but I was probably wrong.

I have memories that are good but they are hard to dwell on right now. The trips to Vegas, the trip to New York the week before he got sick. Was I better to him than I think? I understand now that we never know when something like this will happen. The day he came home from the hospital after the first two weeks there, I hugged him and told him how glad I was to have him home. I remember that he looked so puzzled. I didn't do things like that. I hardly remember those three days. One does not realize how important time like that is when it is happening.

John often told me he loved me. I could never accept that and kept telling him that he told me too often. Do I now know that I was wrong or is it more guilt? When he "awoke" for that hour the other night, I told him how much I love him. He didn't say that he loved me but I never thought of it until he said "I love you, too" to his mother. I could have said "Tell me that," but it never entered my mind. I wish I had.

I cannot believe the pain that this all is. I never dreamed that it could be this bad. Almost every waking moment is spent in sadness. I want to cry even more than I do. The person whom I always turned to in crisis is not here to help. He is not here to talk to. The thought that comes into my head is that I wonder if he ever told Lois that she could tell me things that he said. But did he really ever say anything that I really did not know?

All those who lose those that they deeply love must go through what I am going through. No one can understand unless they have borne this burden. I can only begin to understand how my mother felt when Dad was so sick and when he died after 54 years together. No wonder she put her head in the oven. I think that I understand how she felt and feels, but I know that I really have no idea.

7

Perhaps some of my thoughts are tempered by the fact that I am not sure if I have the time in my life left to even begin to recover from this. Larry says that you never totally recover and I can understand that. He has done well in about 3 years but he knows that he has a lifetime ahead of him. I don't believe that I have that. I seldom say that I am going to get sick. Only that if I do... Is that denial? I believe that my chances of not getting this disease are low. My T cells continue to go down and the stress of the past two months....

Yet, I do hold out some hope, however slight. I will go on for as long as I can. One day there was no cure for polio and the next day there was. It could happen.

John's love will remain with me. I will try to take him home if we can get the 24 hour care that Neal spoke to me about. I owe him that because it is the one thing he wanted.

I wonder what really is in his mind. He smiled today when he bit down on the stick in his mouth. I think he looked at the little stuffed King that I won him at the Excalibur on what may have been our very best vacation. My God, I wonder, what if his thoughts are still totally real? How awful it must be, how frustrating to not be able to get them out.

John wanted to buy Final Exit but I got him to put it off. Now, even the knowledge would do him no good. I don't think that I could do anything to end his life. Yet if he was in terrible pain and suffering, perhaps I could. Of course, I can not tell you that.

I admit that I am afraid. Afraid of the fact that I will lose John. Afraid of the fact that no one will be there to feed me ices and hold my hand every day. But I still thank God, in a sense, that John is going first. If he loves me as much as our friends believe—and I believe that they are right, he might have suffered much more than I am if he had to watch me go through this. Until he found out that he was positive, with low T cells, we always believed that I would go first. We were even comfortable with that because we knew that he would be a far better nurse than I could ever be. He would wait on me hand and foot when I was sick and never, ever had a single complaint.

I wish so much that I had treated John better. I know that he forgives me and that makes it a tiny speck easier to take. I am not sure that I will ever understand his love for me. I pray that one day I will understand how I really feel about him.

What strength I have, I thank God for helping me to survive this. It amazes me that I absolutely believe that there is no life after death, yet put so much faith in the Lord over these years. That is a subject for another time.

the first time

Damn you!
How dare you go?
Anger.
"They" say you feel anger
I do.
I do, now, for the first time.
I don't even feel like crying
At the moment.
I don't feel good
and you're not here
to take care of me.
I'm so lonely
So alone
and you're not here
and you never will be
and I hate that.
I hate you for leaving ?

Dearest Bob,

We're so sorry about your loss – John was a wonderful person – He did a lot, for many so he had a big impact on may lives – I feel very fortunate(sp) to have known him – I know it will be hard but always remember the good times – We loved the trip you took out here with us. Life has many ups & downs. I'm sure he'll walk just beyond the moon & stop & wait for you – You will see each other again –

Love always
Mary & Ken
& boys

10

Tea & Us

Another feeling of loss
I don't feel well
fever, bad headache, tension
take a pill
try tv
go to bed
But there's no one here
No one to make my tea
to make me feel better
No one who cares
and never, ever complains.
Those 4 a.m. mornings when
I woke up sick
If I woke him a thousand times
Never a bad word
Never a complaint
Only caring how I felt
All those years
of making sure I got
better
all those mornings.
My soothing cup of tea
isn't the same
anymore.

AIDS/Mother

Who the Hell am I to question?
I think that you can't hurt
as bad as I do.
You never spent 24 hours of every day
with him.
Not since I was with him.
You still have your love
there with you
Mine is gone
How can you know my pain?
You don't have the lonely nights
the empty days
You have someone to hold your hand
to kiss you good night
to love you, still.
You have love
I only have memories
and sadness.
How can you understand my pain?
Why do you cry?
I loved your son
I loved him so much.

Tears

The tears come at the strangest times
They do not come with the clouds or the sun
They do not come in times of familiar things
In the midst of a conversation;
When someone asks how I'm doing;
Just when I walk through the square.

The tears come at night when it is time to go home;
The sadness sneaks into your soul when you're not looking'
I did not understand the soul
until mine felt so empty one day.

I want to talk to you;
I want to hold your hand
You can be sick again
just be here; with me.

I miss you to the deepest parts of my being
and the only person whom I would tell about
feelings that deep is not here for me to tell.

You would want me to go on
But how am I supposed to do that
When the only person that I care about
will never be here again.

Tell me about memories but
They will not be enough. I know.

H....holiday

Easter
holiday
tears
more tears
I look up
he's not there
not in the choir
I try so hard
but the tears come
Faith
So tested
God
Why
My pew is empty
Where is the meaning
of today
My grief is too much
This was our holiday
No one to share
No one to care
I sing the hymns
As I cry
And at the end
I just want to run
Run away from all of them
They're not him
They can't feel like I do
I want to run away
My head pounds
As I cry and wonder
Will it ever get better?

Short Takes—Sweet Vinegar

New Year's Eve...1973...The Citadel Bar...Boston.

It was close to midnight. My best friend Larry and his other half Rick and I were out to welcome in another new year together. I remember thinking that somehow 1974 was going to be a better year.

The waiter came around with a small bottle of Asti Spumonti which was supposed to be used for each of us to have our own 'Champagne toast.' Each of those at the table opened his and drank it at the stroke of midnight. I didn't open mine; stealing my New Year's drink from Larry.

"I'm saving this," I said, "for the night I get 'married.' "

That bottle moved from apartment to apartment with me. When I moved into the first floor on Winslow Avenue, I put it high atop the mantle and there it stayed.

In 1982, a year after I met John, we were still debating the nature of our relationship (of course, we were still doing that 10 years later). The circumstances can be described in another story, but after a long teary conversation, we agreed to become a couple—"lovers" is the correct term, even though it offends some in straight society.

I went over to the mantle and took down that bottle that had stood there for eight years. The champagne glasses came out of the china closet. We were both pretty happy to have finally made the decision.

I poured the 'champagne' into the glasses. "To our future." We toasted and took a big swig. John looked at me and I back at him. We both must have had a strange look on our faces. That infamous bottle had sat just a bit too long. It was a pretty bitter glass of vinegar.

We laughed and dumped out the remainder. It was the thought that counted.

I still have the bottle. It doesn't go anywhere as long as I'm around. Vinegar never tasted so sweet.

Grief Group

Called Dave
Sorry that after 10 years of waiting
I can't keep my engagement with
Your family
For dinner.
I'm desperate...falling apart
Have to go to first night
of Grief support group.
He calls me a name
Says, go, go, go.
No one looks happy
Tissues on the table
I look better than most
One other guy
What are they on?
Widows
Can I fit here?
We have the same problem
I need these people.
Give and take
Doesn't look quite right
Please help me.
"Lisa will be right here and
We'll start."
Entrance.
"We're sorry but the Omega Group
after 14 years of wonderful success
will cease to exist
the end of June.
Want to talk now?"

None Now

Excitement!
Enthusiasm!
Life!
I wish.
They are not there
I have lost them
My grief replaces
The great things of my life.
When he was down
I had enthusiasm for both of us
Excitement to spare.
None now.
There is little of me that cares
My sadness shoves all else aside
The room is full but of things
That I wish were not there.
Life was my very best friend
Now I don't really like him.
I dream; I pray
for life that I care about
for the good times
for the times that I told him
Life is all about.
There is
A split second; a moment
When I don't feel awful
An unexpected smile
I hope that I have not lost
Excitement
Enthusiasm
Life
There is a dim voice somewhere within
Trying to tell me
They are only misplaced
for a time.

Can't Finish

He left one month ago today
Not possible
Seems like yesterday
Seems like forever
The tears are a little drier
But the emptiness remains
The overwhelmed feeling begins anew
As I write
My eyes tear and I wonder how
I can ever live without him
Shouldn't have started this
Can't write
Damn
I miss you
Wish
You'd come back.
I love you.

The Games We Played

We never played a lot of board games over the years. Although there were a number of them carefully stored away in the drawers under the china closet, they seldom came out. We were always on the go. I wasn't one for sitting down and playing a leisurely game.

But that's hiding what may have been the real reason that we did not play very often. I'm competitive and I always won. Period. Maybe I tried too hard. I attacked any game that John and I played with the same spirit that I always went after life. I had to win and I always did.

We would play cribbage and he would win a game or two, but I would win the most. We played chess on a few occasions where we were pretty evenly matched. I was so thrilled when I pulled out a game that he had virtually won. I think that we both really enjoyed backgammon and John probably could have beaten most people. But not me. So we didn't play too often.

John hated the fact that I took the games so seriously. He might not have cared at all about losing. It was just my need to win that irked him. I was irritated that he was irritated that I had to win. The board games pretty much stayed in the drawer.

One night, sometime in our last (that's tough to say) year together, we spent a night playing Scrabble. Of course, we had played on a number of occasions, often pretty close games, with me coming out, as usual, on the winning end.

That night, the score kept going back and forth. We were both either hoarding our Q's and Z's or got stuck with them and their big points. Neither one of us even had the required 7 pieces left on our holders when I managed to make some word that got me about 23 points. That put me up enough to pretty much end the game for the night.

John sat quietly looking at the board. Usually, I would have bitched about a time limit but it was going to be his last move, if he had one. I couldn't complain, I had the game won.

Out came his Z or his Q, I wish I could remember, put down on the board to make some really stupid 3 letter word. It just happened to be on the triple word score box and it just happened to be one of the highest scoring letters in the game. Seems to me that we even had to look up his stupid word in the dictionary.

Game. Set. Match. John had won his first Scrabble game. It was the only time I ever remember laughing and generally being thrilled with someone else winning.

It was to be our last game of Scrabble. That's o.k. I still smile when I think of the surprise I got when he yanked that win right out from under me.

It may have been the only time in my life when losing gave me such pleasure.

I Have Not Been This Way Before

In a room at Carl's Guest House
Where we spent so many happy days
And a few not so good
But we always enjoyed our times there
In a room at the Cape
Perhaps the only room where we never slept
Together
Feeling so lonely
Empty
More emotions than I am able to understand
How can I miss you so
Yet want someone to hold me close?
No one can fill your place
Not ever.
Contradiction...or is it?
My loneliness is so deep
Only the touch of another person
Could even slightly fill the vacuum
That exists in my being without you.
I feel the guilt of wondering
If it is truly you that I miss
Or the idea of someone being there.
I know
This is all a part of us
Us, We, You, I
The us is no longer
I do not understand
So much
The burden upon my being
Weighs me down.
Heavy laden and not knowing
What Life has in store for me.
Not knowing
What I have in store for me
I fear the future
The burden upon me
Is so heavy.

They Are Not Burdened

My friends are as good as people can be
Where would I be without them during this time?
I would not be; I would not be at all.
The agony of grief is made slightly more bearable
By these people who keep taking the time to care.
Their best comes out.
I had hoped that would be true
Lord, how it is truth.
My dearest friends have been there for me
So, too, have those whom I hardly know.
The nurses who took care of him
Like he was one of their own
And me
As if I was another special patient.
I burden some of my friends with my story
And they are not burdened.
I am afraid and they comfort me
I cry and they touch simply.
Call me anytime; Come for dinner
Tea is ready!
Stay here!
How are you doing?
Are you ok?
Are you really ok?
Sis calls to check on me
Mom says "Give me a call"
Larry's mom waits on the front porch
Just to hug me hello
After her triple by-pass.
"That's your key now," says Grace
Of the one he carried all of his life.
An old man comes to the office to tell me:
What a wonderful funeral.
He didn't know John.
Read about him and was afraid that no one
Would come, because of AIDS.
Carl drives two hours plus for a ten minute
Visit at the wake.
People are so good, they care, reach out

Despite the fact that I have no desire
to go on
No real feelings for anything
I will not throw in the towel
I will not give up
These people don't deserve for me to let them down
For every kindness that I write
There are a hundred more.
I can't let them down.
Not today.

Just a reminder...
to keep your pet healthy,
Call us today!

Printed in U.S.A.   0392

From: Kelsey/schlea
pe

Our records indicate
that _____ is due
for the following:

☐ Annual Vaccination
☐ Rabies Vaccination
☐ Dental Examination
☐ Fecal Check (Bring stool sample)
☐ Heartworm Check
☐ _____

Phone 545-8921 Date Apr 5.
Please call for an appointment today!

TO: Babby who
has h.i.v. pasative
I am so sorry that
you have it.

23

stories of the good times

Write in grief
Write in temper
Write in anger.
Where was le plume
When times were great?
Why don't we sit down
Write those happy thoughts on paper?
When the moment has passed
Will I be able to bring it back?
While the mind grieves
Wondering about the future
What time shall we reach back to remember
All the fine moments that we set aside
Are only the anger, the grief, the sadness
Written in stone?
Wish I had written down stories of the good times
We shall reach into the wells of the soul and find
Memories of a good life.

Short Takes—You Don't Know All

You may know your other half better than anyone in the world, but you don't know everything.

Several weeks after the funeral, I was cleaning our bedroom. On the top shelf, I saw what looked like a black kerchief hanging down. It did not look familiar and I gave it a yank.

Down came the silky material, raining a deck of tarot cards on my head. I had never seen them before and I have no idea if he ever used them or how they got there.

* * *

One morning, about a year ago, we were both in the bathroom. We had lived on Madison Street for about 6 years. I was shaving while John was in the shower. I grabbed a can of shave cream.

(I mentioned earlier that we rent out rooms in the house, but share the bath.)

"John, do you know that I have never bought a can of shave cream since the day we moved in here? I wonder if the tenants have ever noticed?"

The reply came, "I haven't bought toothpaste in 6 years."

* * *

Cleaning out his jewelry box, I found a name written on a small slip of paper that I had never heard. There was a phone number and address with it. I thought, quite seriously, of calling to see whom this could possibly be.

I crumpled the note and threw it away.

* * *

* * *

Fifteen minutes before the starting hour of the wake for John, a strange looking, kind of raggy older woman came into the funeral home. There was no one else there. I honestly thought that a street person had wandered in, but I didn't say a word. She did look vaguely familiar.

She stood for a minute and then walked slowly over to the casket and kneeled. She got up and saw me standing across the room.

"Oh, did you know John?" she asked.

I would like to have seen the look on my face.

"He was such a nice young man."

I still hadn't the foggiest idea of who this lady could be.

"He used to come up to our office all the time to mail out all those envelopes. He was such a nice young man. It's so sad."

It sunk in. I recognized her.

She was the lady who cleaned the office at Neal Insurance. John took all of our campaign and AIDS Committee mailings there. We paid the postage and they let us run them through their machine.

She liked John enough to come to his wake. She had no idea what I was doing there.

The Better Day

An empty spot that I can't describe
Is within me in a place that I can't point out.
I get through the day without a pill
And get more work done but still the feeling
Remains without apt description.
Someone asks, "Did you have a better day?"
Yes.
I think so.
Did I?
What is better?
There were no tears so far this day
The pain did not feel quite like that dagger
Through my heart.
The emptiness within did not subside
My loss is no less
Will it ever be?
There was a tiny difference today
That I cannot describe.
I can't tell you that today was any better
It was not the same
Patience, they tell me
Time will help.
I do not have the patience
I do not know if I have the time
The missing part of me will not return
Faith
Friends who care keep me together
What I need
Is not to be found here today.
The empty space
Is still just there.

Dear Bobby, Hope you feel good. I feel fine. Hope you feel good. I feel fine. Bobby are you sad that you might die. Circle.

(Yes) or (No.) please write me back. I don't want you to die. please don't get mad at me. I am writing becuse I Love you. And I Love you very very much. Do you love me. Circle

(Yes) or ~~No.~~

I Love you.

Love
Kelse

*Kelsey is the author's eight year old great niece.

Two Barrel Hit

Going through the hell of Grief
Trying to recover
Trying to understand
And I get hit again
With the realization that
My T-cells have fallen
"Into my shoes"
As one friend called it.
I want to live
This life is very good
I'm not ready to be sick
or leave.
Despite my raw emotions
After losing the one I love
My physical condition feels good
I can't be that sick
I'm not ready, you know.
No one is.
There are some who live a long time
After this point
I don't know where I am going
What the future holds.
A short time ago I thought
That I had a few years
Now, that's not very sure.
I'm scared
I'm scared of dealing with both.
My faith will be tried today
and tomorrow and the next day.
I hope my faith and my friends will
Help get me through
For a long time.

Grief 101

I knew Grief
I'd met him before
Aunt Nellie died,
Grandma and Grandpa Lamb died
A long time ago
I said good-bye.

I knew Grief, already
He's a busy guy
My nephew Steven was hit by lightning
I cried on the plane
I shook at the casket
I came home.

My good friend Pye died
I cried...I even went to the funeral
Good man at 42
I still think of him.
He gave me the first $3 for my business
It's still on the wall.

Dad died.
I knew it was coming and I was sad
I tried to keep Mom together and
I was strong. I kissed him good-bye
and cried.
I think of him.
Sometimes I wonder why
I did not grieve for him more
Wondering if I'm cold.

Then John died.
I can't write...I'm going to cry again.
How can it hurt this bad?
It hurt this bad before he left me
I know now that we have a soul
Somewhere deep inside
For I have found mine
and there is such pain
and my soul cries
and my soul cries
and I cry.

Dear Bobby
I hope you feel
good, I like you.
You are nice to
people. hope you
don't die.

I Love
You
kelse
y

nel

aw

cool

dd

I Love
you.

Love
kelsey

31

Christmas Bills

That year, things were going real well at the News. Business was so good that I could hardly keep up with it. At the houses I owned, we had at least 2 applicants for every available room. Cash flow was the best it had ever been in my life. We were both enjoying it; buying what we wanted when we headed off to our favorite haunt...the mall.

Even then, John was not one for stretching his money very far. As soon as there was a little extra he would go out and buy something he did not need. Or more likely something special for me. A year after we were together, he went out and got the shaft on buying a new van. The truth was, he wanted me to have it for the paper. He ended up voluntarily having it repossessed. But he tried.

It was sometime in October when I got the idea for his Christmas present. I loved surprises and I knew that this idea would floor him on Christmas morning.

Getting it together would not be easy. I would have to sneak aside the money a little at a time with a check here for expenses or one there for delivery. Then I had to go to the bank each time and ask for the checks to be cashed in my special way. I got a few looks but the money came together slowly. I only got all of it a few days before Christmas.

I also had to find good places to hide it. If John had accidentally come across the cash, he would really have wondered if I was going nuts. I kept it in a number of strange places.

On Christmas Eve, I did the final wrapping. The 1-foot by 1-foot box was not heavy enough. In went 30 rolls of pennies. It was now at least heavy enough to throw off any suspicion of what was in there. Actually, I don't think anyone would have suspected this gift.

On Christmas morning, I played Santa. We had opened all of our "stocking stuffers" and all of our presents for each other. I've lost track of what he gave me for the big present that year. The brightly wrapped box at the back of the tree finally came out.

John lifted it, shook it, and gave me a strange look.

"What could be so heavy and rattly on the bottom of the box?"

He unwrapped it slowly. On top was a layer of tissue paper with a few crumpled up dollar bills on top of it. He took out the 3 or 4 dollars.

"Nice touch, now what's really in here?"

The layer of tissue came up and there was a complete layer of green, crumpled, one dollar bills. John just looked over at me. He was getting suspicious.

He took out the bills, uncrumpled them carefully and put them on the floor. The next layer of tissue was removed to reveal another layer of crumply one dollar bills. No comment. He looked at me, took the bills out, smoothed them into a nice pile on the floor.

When he got down to the third layer, his eyes started to get a bit bigger. He knew something was up. After this layer, the ones did not get un-crumpled, only removed and put on the living room floor where the pile was beginning to grow.

"What are you doing?" he asked in a semi-quizzical way. "There's got to be 3 or 4 hundred dollars in this box."

I told him to "just keep going." There was no argument there.

The layers of tissue kept revealing more crumpled bills, all dollar bills that is. The pile on the floor got very big and so did John's smile.

He got to the bottom of the box and found the 30 rolls of pennies. Then he sat on the floor and flattened out every single dollar bill. As he counted, he kept saying, "I should kill you" and "You shouldn't have done this." He kept neatly putting those bills together, though. His smile kept growing with the fistfuls of dollars.

Each time that John passed another hundred dollar mark, he would look over at me and squint his eyes. I could feel that he was holding in his glee as much as he could.

Nine hundred ninety six. By now he had guessed how many were there. "997, 998, 999, one thousand dollars!"

I think that was the most exciting gift that John Carabineris ever got, since I never did get to buy him his Lincoln Continental.

He told the world about that crazy gift. Whenever I would note that I had given him a thousand dollars for Christmas, he would correct me. I gave him a thousand fifteen.

You had to include the pennies.

Suddenly

Double punch
I lose the man I love
Then
A month later
When I have not even truly thought of recovery
I find that my time may be short
A month ago I was worried about my
Bad attitude of thinking I may only
Have a couple of years
Now, I consider whether I will see 6 months.
How can this be?
Have I denied it all this time?
Yes.
For good reason.
John was here
And then he was sick
He needed me
We had each other.
My own worries did not count
We had each other
Even
If we did not appreciate what we had.
But I think we did.
And now John is gone
And the loneliness today
Is hardly thought of in my mind.
Now, I suddenly have to worry about me.
I know that my grief is not over
It is but temporarily set aside
While I consider the ramifications
of 43 little T cells.
I consider the future
Whatever there will be of it.
Suddenly
So little time
I must use it well.
Hello up There
I need your help.

Dear Bobby I hope you are feeling oaky. Are you sad that Jhon died circle.

Yes or NO

hope you are feeling oaky there

Love
Kelsey

COOL

WOW

are you sad

circle

Love

Yes or No

35

Newspaperman's Dreams

Tomorrow
I'll buy the Sunday *Globe* again
Read a bit of it perhaps
Like I used to do over coffee
Every Sunday
At the bakery for so many years.
The Travel section used to be our dreams
And our realities as we flew off
To Phoenix
Las Vegas,
Orlando
New York City
Atlanta
Phoenix, again
Los Angeles
And a hundred other places in my/our minds.
The Arts & Films section
Sent us off to the movies
Served as a reminder to call the agent
And reserve our press tickets
For the next musical coming
To town.
Reading through the Business section
Looking for a house in Real Estate
I'd sit with him over coffee each week
After church.
He would read some too.
Probably out of boredom while I delved deeply
Into the pages.
The Sunday *Globe* sits quietly on the table
Then quietly on the couch at home.
There is no good reason to read it today.
No one to talk to about what I've read.
The dreams of travel are not dreams anymore
No movies to be seen together
All those years of loving my Sunday paper
Once in a while I even managed to bring
The New York Times home on Sunday
Not today.
Newspaper dreams are gone
For now.

Tears on Leaving

So many of us are leaving you
Our time is short in this realm
If Ronald Reagan had cared
That so many of us were leaving
back then
Maybe more of us could stay.
Lots of us don't even know
But I do.
And so do many of my friends
Those I sit with at the bar
They know.
Some just avoid it.
I've known for 7 years
John knew for less than 3.
John is gone.
So many are going so fast
To hell with the Quilt as
It grows too fast.
Do you understand what is happening?
Do only those who have lost a lover,
a brother, a sister, or two dozen friends
Understand?
We are leaving you so fast
Every day
Every week
So many for you to wish farewell
So many to wish you good-by.
I do not want to leave you
None of us do.
Do you understand?
Washington seems to have no idea
Or don't enough of us vote?
We will miss you.

"Once, I Had A Wonderful Day"

We used to kid that if we counted the number of times that we separated, our relationship would really only be a couple of years. That wasn't quite true because our breakups never ended up lasting very long.

John was living in our house on Broadway. He had moved there to watch over things when I had first purchased the house. At that point he was living in his father's building in Chelsea because we needed to live apart "for awhile."

He lived on the second floor for quite a while but we were still having a tough time making a go of it.

One day, I was sitting at home when John showed up, walked in the door and told me, "I'm moving to P'town (Provincetown, at the end of Cape Cod)." Period.

He had his car parked out front, loaded to the roof with everything he could fit. I was floored. We talked for an hour or so. We both cried. He had decided that this was best for both of us. I tried to talk him into staying. But he was determined and he knew that if he did not leave right then, he wouldn't go. I remember him saying, as we talked, "If we only had long talks like this before...." But we were never good at talking things out.

John left for the Cape. I recall going over to Broadway. He had left a lot behind and I had to clean out the room. I remember the feeling very well. The emptiness in me was like he had died. Today, I know that was exactly the feeling. Except then I could go to Provincetown and see him anytime.

I did so on a number of occasions. Once, he was seeing someone for several weeks and what it did to me when I saw him walking down Commercial Street with someone else, I cannot describe. My heart skipped beats that I didn't know it had.

Most of my trips, I would eat where he was working and then we would go out for a drink. Then he would walk back to the guest house with me and it would be time for me to subtly talk him into staying. He didn't always agree, yet most of the time we ended up with each other. I was always worried, but he had a tough time saying No when it came to us being together. All this took place during the summer and fall about the fifth year that we were together.

I continued to visit him in P'town as summer turned to fall and the Christmas season approached. Absence makes the heart grow fonder and we were doing pretty well. He wasn't thinking too much about coming back and I dared not bring it up too often.

Seems that it was the week before Christmas that I went to visit and we spent a few days together. He had not made it up to 'our' annual Christmas party and that bothered me a great deal.

The reason isn't clear to me now, but he wasn't even planning to come up to see his parents for the holidays. It may have been because he didn't have the money to buy his family gifts. That would have bothered him. At that point, he wasn't working very much and was getting only small unemployment checks.

I was not looking forward to being without him on Christmas, and not going to his family's house. It was a wonderful place to be on the holidays. I went home that weekend not a very happy camper. Christmas has been my favorite time of year since I can remember. It was doomed to be a very lonely day.

Christmas Eve must have been on a Thursday that year, because I remember that our bartender friend Mike Markowski was on the front bar at 119. At least I think I remember that.

I wasn't in a very good mood that Christmas Eve. My father was in very poor shape at home and I was alone. I wasn't about to stay home feeling sorry for myself, so it was off to 119 around my usual 11 o'clock arrival.

I walked in the door and plunked myself down at the front of the bar. I started to order a drink. Michael looked at me with a smile on his face. I don't know his exact words, but he basically let me know that someone I should see was sitting down at the other end of the bar.

There was John, sitting with a drink and a smile. I suspected that I tried not to glow from ear to ear, but I remember my heart skipping a beat. It still does when I think of seeing him sitting there.

We went home that night and I don't remember a thing about it.

I did have presents under the tree for him. Maybe I had hoped he would show up or maybe I was planning to bring them to the Cape. Today, I have no idea which, but they were there and we opened them on Christmas morning, with John complaining that he had nothing for me. His presence was enough....

I am so clear on how happy I was that day. I sat beside him on the couch and held his hand. I told him how glad I was that he was there with me. I wished that he would move back home....

I asked if he had ever seen the movie "Hello, Dolly," because I was thinking of a line from that movie that described exactly how I felt right then.

The young man in the movie had met a girl and his friend wondered, what if he never, ever saw her again. The older boy told him, just before bursting into song, it doesn't matter, for "I shall always know that once I had a wonderful day." I told John that this was my "wonderful day." That no matter what else happened, this day would always be so special.

I think he liked hearing that. He was certainly glad to be there with me. We went and surprised my parents and then went off to Danvers, where his whole family was floored when we showed up. It was a wonderful day for all. That Christmas Day was the happiest day of my life. How many people are lucky enough to realize that fact?

That day must have had just as strong an effect on John. I drove down and surprised him on New Year's Eve a week later. The next day, I dropped him off at work as I got ready to drive back to Boston.

He got out of the car. I had my window open, talking to him.

Out of a clear blue sky, he said to me "I've been thinking a lot about what you've said about coming back. I think you'll be happy with my decision." I remember those words exactly. He turned around and walked into the restaurant without another word.

I was floored. It probably took a few minutes for that grin to spread from ear to ear again. I can still feel the happiness of that moment when I think of that day.

John moved home two months later.

postscript

Michael Crawford, a very young actor, spoke that line in "Hello, Dolly." He went on many years later to be the star of "Phantom of the Opera." John performed the song "Music of the Night" (which Crawford made famous) in several shows and kind of made it his theme song (mainly because I loved hearing him sing it). Strange coincidence.

Do Not Go Gently

Feelings that are torn
Unsure of my thoughts
For whom do I grieve?
I miss John so.
All that I do still lacks what he gave
Just his being there
Meant more than I ever knew.
Now
I look at my own life.
Questioning
How much time I have
Knowing
That I should not.
My tears still come at strange times
But now I am not sure when I cry
If those tears are for John
Or for me.
I worry about the future
I admit that I am afraid.
Death may not be a terrible thing
It finds us all
Sickness, incapacity, pain
They are the worry
And who will be there for me?
No lover. But
I am not going gently into that good night
Oh no, not me.
My spirit will return.
I will fight.
He would demand that of me.
Today, I know
There will be a tomorrow.

Bubblehead

The act is not together
The mind doesn't want to quite work
Sometimes the legs are wobbly
The feet don't go where they are supposed to go.
The numbers don't seem to add up right.
Confusion makes me feel like a bubblehead.
I get so damn angry
When I can't put three thoughts together.
Got to make plans to eat dinner with someone
Tonight is the Cancer Society dinner
But it's Wednesday...
The girls at the Mt. Vernon Restaurant
Will be waiting for me
So I'd better go there
Or should I go to the banquet
Where my doctor is getting an award
Which would be better?
Maybe I'll go to both
And only eat a little.
Hello, mind, where are you
I think I miss you
Could you come back for a visit
They've been very short lately.
As has my temper.
Can't stand being alone
Drives me through hell and back
Still, I don't want to answer the phone.
The answering machine light is blinking
I get edgy... now who's on there.
The light's not blinking
Damn, no one called.
Hello, mind
Can we sit down and talk
and maybe
Get it together
Someday soon?

Shakespeare's Lament

Time...my enemy?
No, not really
Yet not my friend
Now, time is so often in my thoughts.
How much is there?
I don't want to think by the day
The future always looked good
Tomorrow is so unsure
Months... years
Where am I going?
I never liked thinking of vacations
Too far ahead
For I knew they would end
And it would be as if only a dream.
Time is unique.
Yesterday, I met my lover at the bar
Eleven years later
Tomorrow
He is gone.
The days go slow.
The years fly.
I try to live each day
I try to smile again
My thoughts go back to time
Be it months or years
That I have spent here
It will really be
tomorrow
So soon.

Short Takes — First Night/Last Day

A lot of folks must have wondered why I wore old black pants and a black cowboy shirt with big red embroidered roses to the cemetery. Not a single person has ever asked.

The night that I met John, I was not the usual me with a suit and tie, which is about all I wore back then, even to the bar. Every once in a while, I would go to the 119 in full cowboy outfit. I had won several really nice shirts at another bar and bought my own black hat. I also had in my new contact lenses. So I really wasn't the Bob that all the folks at the bar were used to seeing. This was kind of a new me; at least for that night.

John was at the door gabbing with Allen, the doorman, and Allen's lover. I knew them both and I knew that I wanted to meet John. I think I said, "Are you going to introduce me to this good looking blond?" Seems to me there was a surprised look on his face. They introduced us. We barely talked that night, but at least I knew his name. I filed it wherever you file those things in your mind for the future.

The future arrived quickly. The next night, August 3rd, 1981, John was sitting on the second stool from the left end at the back bar. It was a Wednesday, so Michael was probably on the bar. We were not close friends back then.

John and I gabbed for quite a while. I wanted to bring him home, so I decided to use the same line that I had often used if I really wanted to get to know someone. I could usually tell by their reaction if they were interested and the line almost always got at least a smile.

I asked, "So, what are you doing for the next six months?"

It was also my way of letting a potential guest know that I wasn't really interested in a one-night stand.

John looked at me quite seriously. No smile. Uh-oh. Was I about to strike out?

"Is that all?"

I had no idea just how serious he was that night.

Ten and a half years later, I wore that same cowboy outfit in which I had said "Hello" to say "Good-bye."

Editor's Forward

AIDS just took a friend from me. I first met John Hedley Carabineris, Jr. a little over two years ago when I moved to Davis Square. John was Assistant Publisher for The Somerville News and I, of course, was busy with The BCN. John was tall, handsome, intelligent, quietly effective and immediately likeable.

The more I learned about this sweet-souled man, the better I thought of him, but it wasn't until we got onto the subject of music one night that I really became excited. Here was someone who loved to sing yet wasn't familiar with my musical passion—early American *fa-so-la* music.

From that moment on, I looked forward to the day when we would lift our voices together in hymns that predate the American Revolution.

But, you know how life is: I was busy, then he was busy and somehow we never connected. Who has time to stop and smell the roses? And then one day, I heard John was gravely ill.

And now he is dead.

Tears won't bring John back, but you can bet my eyes will be filled when I dedicate my favorite songs to him at the next singing. And I hope that somewhere out there—beyond all earthly pains and sorrows—John is singing with me.

Wishing I had stopped to smell the roses,

Dean Wallace

Just Dropped In, Deanna

Some folks cheer me up
I'm not quite sure why
What have they got
To offer?
My very best loved friends are great
They don't always make me smile
or feel better.
There are some special folks
That I can go visit
Anytime.
I leave smiling.
Not best friends,
Just people I know
Do they make other people
Feel good too?
What unique quality do they have
That offers such moments of respite?
I doubt if these fine folks
Know that's why I visit them.
I hope that I make someone
Feel better
When
They need it.

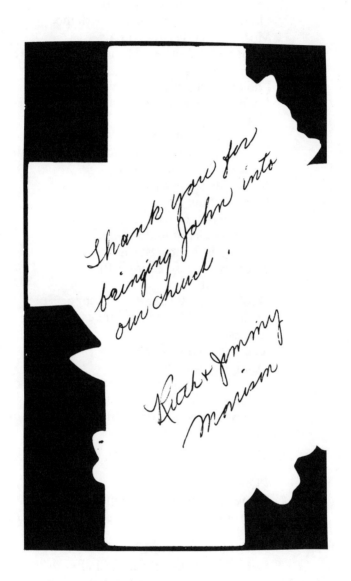

Thank you for
bringing John into
our church.

Kick & Jimmy
Morison

A Place I Do Not Know

I told him as I held his hand
On the last day that he was with me.
Most of what I said that day
Is hidden somewhere in the depths of my mind.
Even now
I do not comprehend the words
My beliefs have not changed
Nor has my faith
Which has kept me going.
Sometimes in a conversation with a friend
Or when I am quietly alone
My words come back to me.
When I think about them
My very innermost me
Simply does not understand.
So, why do I know this is true?
There is nothing after death.
I know that.
Don't ask me how my faith supports me
In these troubled and sad times so well
It does.
There is no life after death.
I told him at least twice
Not out of grief or despair or
Because I wanted him to hear it.
The words came from somewhere inside of me
That I do not know.
"We will be together again some day."
Even as I spoke
I knew
Something unique was happening
That touched me
and
Gave me those words.
Lord, I know there is naught after death.
But my words from that place within
That has no name
are true.
Simply
I cannot understand.

Amen.

Around the Country in Eleven Years

There must be a story in every trip that we went on during those years together. The travels themselves are worthy of a book-length feature.

I remember John attending what was then 'my' annual Christmas party. We had met that August and he was still around, helping me plan the party and cooking for it.

During the party, Jason, a young man whom I had helped out by letting him stay at my house for a few weeks, called. He had somehow found his way to Hawaii and was living there with a guy from the Army. He invited me to visit and stay with them.

Going to Hawaii seemed like a good idea, so I managed to get together enough money to head for the islands. Did it ever enter my mind to take John along? I doubt it. Neither one of us had much money then. He was working for the state and the <u>News</u> wasn't ready to pay for two people...yet. So I made my reservations and went alone.

It wasn't a very good trip. There were many reasons, including six days of rain and the fact that I could not even afford to rent a car. Over the upcoming years, I seldom went on any trips alone. I talked about doing so and went on trips a few days ahead but that was it.

Somewhere in our relationship, I went to Florida alone for what was to be five days. I could not stand it and changed my reservation to come home a day early.

After that, I only traveled alone once, on the trip when John and I were going to visit a friend in Hawaii. I stopped for four days by myself in L.A. and ended up with a four-day migraine. I had to call John to tell him to bring pain pills.

We developed certain things that we did in every city. We seldom visited the bars; there was too much else to do. We did become experts on zoos. Neither one of us was a big zoo fan, but we turned into real pros after a visit to the Miami Zoo. Maybe it was watching a mother gorilla nurse her three-day-old baby. After that, we never missed the zoo in any city we visited.

I love to head off into the sunset. Having a lover who enjoyed the trips as much as I did only made it easier to say "Let's go." The newspaper's barter deal with a travel agency didn't hurt either.

As things got better at the <u>News</u> and money came from renting rooms, we took off every chance we got. I don't know how many times we visited Las Vegas, Phoenix, Orlando, or Ft. Lauderdale. We tried Atlantic City on a number of occasions without winning. Atlanta was a bore. Denver was wonderful when we went to visit my brother. Our two cruises were among our most memorable times.

We were saving up to go back to Hawaii this year.

John and I had plenty of our little tiffs on those trips. When you travel that much, why would being away be any different than being at home? The memories are mostly good ones. We stayed at some flea bag hotels and we stayed at some of the best. We ate at the Hyatt and at Burger King.

Our good friend, Mike Markowski, went with us on several trips. His favorite tourist stops were revolving restaurants. We hit them in L.A., San Diego, and Phoenix. I've lost track of where else we ate as the world turned.

While on the trip to California, we discovered that the rates to Phoenix were so cheap that we decided to fly there from San Diego for a couple of days. Mike and John were all for it. We got to visit my nephew and his family while the our bartender friend headed to the Grand Canyon for a sight seeing tour.

On the day that it was time to go home, we had to head back from San Diego. Remember, we had arrived via L.A. We got to the airport and for some reason, I sent Michael in to get the tickets for our cheapie fare back.

Michael hates to do anything like that, but he agreed, while we were busy doing something outside of the terminal. We were running late. He had the luggage, too.

Michael came flying out of the terminal with the tickets in hand.

"The flight leaves in 10 minutes. We have to hurry or we'll miss the plane!"

That did not make sense to me, since I knew that we had about 45 minutes until our flight left. In the rush, I guessed that I had just looked at the schedule wrong.

We flew along the corridors of the airport, lugging our carry-ons. It was a typical long, long way from the desk to the gate. I kept listening for the announcement that we had missed our flight.

"Last call for Flight 888 to Los Angeles."

Yes, that was our flight.

I looked at my ticket to check the flight number. It hit me. That was our flight. One problem: we were supposed to be returning to Boston via San Diego. I stopped dead in my tracks about 20 feet in front of a running John and Michael.

"Michael, where did you buy tickets for?"

He looked at me, looked at his ticket and his face fell a foot. "Oh, my

God."

Our luggage was carefully checked—and we almost were, too—to Los Angeles instead of San Diego. If I had not for some reason caught that announcement, we would have ended up on the plane to L.A. and missed our flight home. Now, I know why they tell you what flight you're on.

Quickly back to the counter. Could they get our luggage? The plane was at the gate but the girl at the counter would try her best.

She called downstairs. The doors had already been shut. They probably could not do anything. Someone called back. He would try.

Don't ever say that airline people don't try. This young baggage handler for America West got out on the runway before the plane left the loading area, flagged it down and went in and got our luggage.

After many thanks, I went back to the ticket counter and got the tickets for San Diego. After all that, somehow we made the flight.

When it was time to board the flight from San Diego to Boston, we were relieved and ready to go home. But Michael had lost his ticket... A story for another time.

Short Takes—That Day

Perhaps a month or so after John had returned from his move to Phoenix, he was still not feeling very well. I insisted that it was time to go for "the test" (for HIV).

He agreed and got an appointment at Fenway Community Health Center. Two weeks later, he went for the results.

John came into the bedroom, not looking very happy. I knew, but I only guessed part of the story.

"I'm positive."

I quietly reminded him that we really had expected that.

"I have a T-cell count of 86."

I put my arms around him and he cried for the first time in the eight years I had known him.

Dear John —
  While Bob & I were very near
  You let us know by a Tiny Tear
  It's OK, I'm glad your here
  We held your hand, there was no fear
  The three of us knew, it was very clear
  The Lord had plans for one so dear
  He came and drew you very near.

                    I wish for you Peace
                    Joan R.N.

53

Short Takes—Forever

Perhaps a week or two after John had discovered his HIV status and low T-cell count, he was in a little better mood. He took his AZT, etc., faithfully, though he complained about feeling tied to the drugs.

John was still sleeping in the room next door to mine. He had not returned from Phoenix as my Lover, but as a friend. His leaving that time was the only time it was pretty much by mutual agreement. When he came home, I offered him the room at no charge until he could pay for it or get a place on his own.

We were talking back and forth from room to room one day and I told him that he probably should move back into my room. Finances were not great and I could use the money if we could rent his room out.

John came out of his room, looking somewhat solemn. I'm not sure he knew just what he wanted to say...no, I'm sure.

"Since we've both got this thing, maybe we should just stick it out, together."

"Yeah."

His simple statement, my simple answer, guaranteed that we would be together until one of us was gone.

Appreciate

Got up feeling blue this morning
Bad dreams
Might have been about my mortality
Really have no idea
Shook up when I got up
Like after you've been frightened.
Ate my Frosted Flakes
Out of a baggie at the bakery.
Larry ran out, ill
Headed home for a nap.
Called Ma to go pick out flowers
For her teeny garden
Bought dozens for our garden
Planted about a dozen flats
In the yard.
Purple and white.
John and I used to kid about doing that.
Phone rings
Dog is ready at the cleaners
Walked all the way to get her
And walked home again
Thinking as I walked.
Joey may not make it through the night.
David has cancer in his foot.
Charlie was at the bar with pneumonia.
I'm here with my 43 T cells
Gardening and walking the dog up the hill.
I looked up and said to the Sun
Fill me with your strength and power
I want to live forever.
I looked up and felt good.
Appreciate, my friend.
Oh, lucky man!

Dear Pastor Nagle

Your sermon on Sunday was a great one. It made me think a great deal. That's why I'm writing this letter to you.

God loves me and He knows I'm gay.

If there is a Heaven, and I'm not very sure of that, He will be waiting for me with open arms and give me a hug as I enter. God is really something.

I firmly believe that I was born gay. No different from the person who is born left handed or with a lazy eye. No one wrote in the Bible that "he who uses his left hand to scribe shall be called the sinner." If someone had written those words, would we be hearing about 'left hand bashings' or would many not care when people with a lazy eye got sick? I have a feeling those very things would be happening today.

The good men who wrote the words in the Bible had their own hangups. Unfortunately, homosexuality was one of them. But they were but men. God never said "man shall not life down with man, for that is an abomination." Men said that. It is men who still say that today, not God.

I am going to die of AIDS. I have never said that before but there has to be a first time. Perhaps there will be a miracle and I will live to a ripe old age, but I have to accept the fact that only a miracle will save me. I plan to stick around as long as I can.

Being gay is not the most important thing in my life. My life, my family, my friends, helping people are all so much more important. I love people. They are the most wonderful thing that God ever made. He knew what he was doing.

In my own church, I could not be a minister because I am gay. All the good works that I have done, all my love for all people makes no difference. That's wrong. The Catholic church gets away with exactly the same wrong, except they use excuses with women to keep them out.

I do nothing morally wrong when I make love to another man whom I love. I am not sinning. Loving someone truly and dearly, as I loved John Carabineris, could never be a sin in God's eyes. I am no angel, I have sinned in many ways. If I had remained monogamous during our 11 years together, we might both have lived many years.

I'm writing this to you to try to give you, as a pastor and man of God, a better idea of what goes on in the mind of someonewho is gay. I have managed to get through life because of my faith. God has helped to give me the strength, courage and the wisdom that I have needed. If he was not with me right now, the men in the white coats would be coming for me.

I lost the man I loved and discovered that my own time is probably much shorter than I had thought. Only God will get me through this with a little help from my friends. You may need to give my mother a little help.

For some reason many years ago, I started a tradition with myself. Each year, on my birthday, I ask myself, if I could give up being gay and never know that I was gay, would I do so? The answer has always been no. Even now, as this plague threatens to strike me down, I have not changed my mind.

Being gay is normal...to me. Many people have different traits and God does not call them sinners. If, indeed, as studies show, 10% of the world's population is gay, maybe He wanted it that way.

I am telling you all this because I hope it will give you a better understanding of how a homosexual who is happy with himself and has a wonderful relationship with God feels. I do not believe that in my case it is 'Love the sinner, Hate the sin.' My desire to love men, even if many cannot understand it, is no sin.

If I can ever answer any questions for you that would help in your decisions at any conference, please feel free to call upon me. God Bless.

Sincerely yours,

Bob

Robert J. L. Publicover

cc: Rev. Schrader
    Rev. French
    Rev. Colcord

No One Across the Table

Ravioli
Papa Gino's
Alone
Not feeling down or up
Certainly not happy
Not miserable
No tears
On edge
Feeling a little blank
Sitting here
Missing the days
Of dinner out, together
Of dinner in, together
Of back porch bar-b-ques.
For a while I called friends
The meals were better
But don't I have to learn
At some point
To be with me, just me, again?
I suspect it is a process
Learning to be alone
A process that I flunked
Long before I met him.
Tonight
I eat half my meal.
Alone
Is not a game that I play well.

News

SOMERVILLE

"Somerville's Most Widely Read Newspaper"

Dear Kelsey,

Thank you very much for your wonderful letters. It makes me feel very good to know that you care about me.

I am feeling okay right now but I miss John a lot. It is lonesome when I go home from the office at night. I try to do things, like go to a movie but it is not fun without him. I am sad that he died but I know God is taking care of him now.

I am sad that I might die but I do not think about that. I think about being here today with my friends. I think about all of those that I love like you and Mandy and your mommy + daddy.

I hope to visit you some day soon. Please tell your family that I love them all. I am sending you a gift that John gave me that I hope you will like.

Lots of Love

Uncle Bobby

Seven Davis Square • Somerville, MA 02144
666-4010

Stories

The church is old and majestic
In Boston's Copley Square
Came to the AIDS Healing Service
On a quiet Tuesday night
The choir sings
The minister speaks
I am not the only one with tears.
AIDS Healing Service.
So many go to the altar rail
The "laying on of hands"
Begins
So many stories here
One man helps a younger man
Down the aisle
Slowly with his cane
A man leads a woman, so slowly
I'm surprised by so many women
And so many tears
Many faces are not familiar
Yet
There is a quiet comfort here
He is young
She is old
A grey-haired lady spots a friend
Hurries across the altar
To embrace
So many stories here
Pain
Sorrow
The young man in his frock
Looks like a disciple
Solemn
Quiet
Sobbing somewhere
All of us so different
So alike
We all are here with our stories
That few will hear
But too many know
Here
For the touch
Of God's grace.

On the Road to Vegas

We had purchased the package plan to Vegas World three years ago. We just never got around to going. For various reasons the trip just kept getting put off. We had been there several times and always enjoyed our trips.

This package plan included $1,000 in gambling stakes. It was their silver dollars and 'even money', which meant if you bet one of their $5 chips, you got back a real $5 chip and they took yours. It was a good deal that included two nights at the hotel. If you bet right (they told you how), you could get all the money that you had paid for the trip back.

They figured, of course, that you would then gamble that and more. They were usually correct.

Our plan had run out nearly two years before but I sat down one day and wrote them a letter on Somerville AIDS Committee stationery explaining that the person who had purchased the plan was ill. Would it be possible to still use it?

We got a phone call three days later. "Come on out to see us and use your package plan...but we don't have any rooms." That was fine. We wanted to stay at the new Excaliber anyway.

We made reservations. The week before we were scheduled to go, John began running a fever. His doctor put him in the hospital. They could not find anything wrong. He got out the day before we were due to fly to Las Vegas.

John was going on that trip, come Hell or high water. We got to the airport on time.

The Excaliber, built like an ancient castle, was an experience. Jugglers, clowns, musicians were all over the halls until late at night. The $3.99 buffet filled you to the brim if you could stand waiting in line.

Did I mention that we both won when we picked up our money at Vegas World? Good start.

On the floor where the restaurants and much of the entertainment was located, there were lots of shops with items ranging from souvenir pencils to outrageous crystal pieces.

John spotted a puppet that you could work with your hands, about two feet tall. The man showing it was great and John wanted one. The base price for this guy, whom we named 'Sherwood', was about $30. Then came the outfit he wore, and a hat and a mustache. I think that little Sherwood came to about a hundred bucks. John had a ball wandering the casinos with Sherwood waving to the world. It was questionable who was the center of attention.

The whole point of this story begins in a little area that we ran into about the same time as we got Sherwood. There were two artists painting charcoal portraits. Lots of samples were posted in their spaces. All of them were excellent, as were the portraits that both were working on at the time we stopped by.

I remembered the wake of a Somerville friend who had died of AIDS a year or so ago. His family had put up a portrait that had been most likely painted by one of the artists in Provincetown. Bob looked so fine and healthy.

I am not sure if I ever told John the real reason that I thought a portrait might be nice. I was always honest with him, but I really don't remember how blunt I was in this instance.

We talked about it and we decided that the portrait, which cost less than Sherwood, would be something great for his mother. It could be a combination birthday/Christmas present. He set up an appointment for the next morning.

I strolled by a few times watching the artist take about an hour to draw the portrait that John would bring home to Mom. John sat like a stone. His blue eyes must have caught the special attention of this artist because they shine in the portrait.

That Vegas vacation was one of the best times we ever had. We hated to come home. We had fun. Sherwood, the portrait, and winning at gambling all made for a special time.

That portrait hangs in a proud spot on Grace's dining room wall. I was never thrilled with it, but neither was I unhappy. John's charcoal likeness never got to the wake. I'm not sure why. Perhaps I never thought of suggesting that his parents bring it. Maybe I just wanted people to see John as he looked that day.

To this day, looking at the picture on the wall bothers me. On Easter, I ended upstairs in tears after sitting looking at him. That was only three weeks after the funeral, and I wasn't ready.

Whether or not I ever told John my real reason for having that portrait done does not matter. He knew. It never served the purpose for which it was bought, but I suspect that his mother will treasure it forever.

Sometimes your plans work out O.K. after all.

Collision

It seems like I live in two different worlds
One of loneliness and grief and missing
Another of having moments where I am a different person
A person who is making it on my own
Trying to get my life together
Looking around
Thinking about making love
Going out to the bar
Sitting on the front steps at 2 a.m.
Crying.
I miss him so.
Going out and meeting someone
Making love
A trip to the cemetery with Mom
Leaving a yellow rose for each of us
Shedding a tear as I leave his pink cap
Writing poetry about our life together
Stories so that others will understand our love
And to help others survive in their grief.
Writing a personal classified ad
To meet someone
Getting aggravated that my personal message
won't record
Scared of the long weekend coming up
Never spent one alone
Making plans to keep busy
Missing him
Will I meet someone?
Should I try?
Two worlds
They keep colliding.

Scattered Thoughts in the Office

Making a visit to the doldrums today
And the ride is rocky
Last day of a three-day weekend
Keeping a list of things to do
To keep busy
To keep my mind occupied.
Two months yesterday and the day
Didn't seem that much different.
Joey's wake. I brought a rose.
Cleaned house and kept finding things
That I really didn't need to find.
Reminders that bring back more than you want
Getting through it though
Knowing that's for just so long
So off to the office on this holiday
Suddenly, no warning, the tears come
Nothing happened to set them flowing
Overwhelmed
Not sure by what
I take out his photo to hold.
Sadness, loneliness, emptiness
I still miss you so.
I want to write a story
But nothing inspires
Your desk sits there, empty
I know how it feels
The box of items for your Quilt panel
Sits coldly on your chair.
I'm not happy
I was doing pretty well
Maybe I was almost ready to say Good-by.
But
No.

too young

I feel an anger building within me
That had been hidden away
Unseen, unknown, but there
Like the virus
Suddenly, set off by a minor incident
It preys on my mind.
They are sick too young
They are dying too young
Lives are not being fulfilled
Young men should not die
There is so much ahead
My four decades don't seem like much
Until I think of Michael who was 28
When he died.
Charlie and Shamus and Rick
all sick and
Not yet 30 years of life.
They know that the days ahead
May not be many
Like me
I've had all these years that they will never see
John was 31
I never thought of him as that young
In our 11 years together
Too young to die.
With whom shall I be angry?
God?
This is not his doing
Society?
No, it is not your fault.
I am bitter as these good young men die
In a one-sided war
That finds no end
I am angry.
The virus that takes men too young
Incurs my wrath
How can one be angry with a virus?
I have not found a way.
My anger remains
And grows.

Sunshine

Sunny days
Don't have the flavor that they had before
But as they come along in the Spring
Each one of them is a tiny speck better.
Out for a walk
Business or pleasure
Out in the garden
Before the sore bones
Tell me that I did too much.
The bright ball of yellow
Has a quality of healing
Whatever my mood
I feel just a little happier
Out there in the light
On a sunny day.
Yes, I wish you were here with me
On a walk through the Public Gardens
Or just a block away for our cup of cappucino
You're not.
I think of you often
The memories are a little more mellow
A bit softer
The smiles a mite quicker
When the sun
Shines.

The Great Political Campaign
(Or) A Lesson I Got in Loyalty and Love

It was a candidate for Mayor who had urged me to run for Alderman-at-Large two years before I did. It was the same guy who ended up as one of my opponents in the race.

More than one of the four elected Aldermen-at-Large were not making me very happy with their actions. They had been around too long, in my opinion, and a change might be in order.

I considered running nearly a year before the election. There wasn't a great deal of talk about the subject between John and me, at least not that I remember. Seems that there were probably a lot of one-sided conversations where I would talk about the possibility. The decision was made that I would decide if I should run sometime after we returned from Hawaii in January.

Many friends were consulted about the possibility and John was usually there. He never said much but he always listened intently. Even that surprised me. John was not one to get involved in politics. Too many people. Too many crowded rooms. Crowds were one of his least favorite things in the world.

Many a Wednesday night was spent at our regular Mt. Vernon Restaurant haunt, talking about politics with the manager. John told me later, "Half the time, I don't know what you and Tom are talking about, but I sure love to listen. I get a lot out of it."

When I first considered running, I started a card file. I determined that if I could not get 1,000 cards of potential votes in the file, there was no sense in seeking the office. I got the cards.

Right after I got home from Hawaii, I told John that I had decided to run. Somehow, he was not surprised. Sometimes, he knew me better than I did.

I make no bones about the fact that I knew quite well that this could be my last healthy chance to run and John's last shot at being there to help. We never said that to each other but we both knew.

We got out nearly a thousand invitations to the $50-a-ticket fund raiser at the Mt. Vernon in April. The returns were not bad, but we had no idea how many would actually come. We were both petrified that no one would show. I took it for granted that John would use his karaoke and sing. He did.

A large number showed up at the door, including his always-loyal parents. The night was a real success, even beyond our expectations.

John was as nervous as usual, but he sang as well as ever, and many people commented favorably. He was happy.

Next came the announcement party in June. That was planned too close to the big fund raiser, and the crowd wasn't too good. We were disappointed but took it in stride. John performed his songs for the small crowd and really saved the night. I hope he realized that fact.

Meanwhile, summer came and went. John took care of getting all the information about bulk mailing. There were to be nearly 7,000 letters in each mailing. He typed and typed—more lists than you can imagine.

We decided to have a breakfast, after the owner of a Davis Square restaurant offered us the space. Out went more fund raising letters. I explained to John that this had never been done before in the Square. We didn't know what would happen at 8 a.m. on a Monday morning.

At 8:15, there was one person in the half of the restaurant that we were using. John set up the trusty karaoke in the corner, looking like he would have a heart attack, he was so nervous, but willing to sing to one person if he had to do so. An hour later, he was singing his heart out to a full house, with not a seat available. I was waiting on and cleaning up the tables as fast as I could.

It was a very good morning. We left Mike's with a big smile, knowing that somehow we had again pulled off a success. The line of the day was again, "What a beautiful voice. I didn't know that John could sing." I think he was stealing my show and I didn't know it.

Maria Curtatone, the other Mayoral candidate, was there and she raved about him. She asked if he was available for her coffee parties. I said he was and told her to talk to him. They arranged a price. John had his first paid "gig" and was ecstatic. He sang for her campaign at several coffee parties.

Should I mention that he was now on disability? I handled John's money but it wasn't very much. He still did tons of work at the News even if I always complained that he was never doing enough. John's T cell count at this point was down to 23. The AZT didn't appear to be doing much. He had spent a week in the hospital in August with the flu.

The entertainer in John was thrilled with the work from Maria. He entertained at her parties for Senior citizens and made $35 for each one. He told me that he wanted a few items for the karaoke. I let him charge them on my MasterCard.

He never did turn any profit on those parties. But he was happy. He was going to hide the day that the bill for the new music equipment arrived. It came to over $400. Every last penny was dutifully paid back to me.

On the last day to take out papers to run for office, John Buonomo, who had spent $70,000 running very strongly but unsuccessfully for Mayor two years earlier, took out papers for Alderman-at-Large. I knew the race was over, but I was not about to quit. I would give it my best shot.

John and I worked harder and harder on getting the bulk mailing ready, on delivering door-to-door, on arranging for poll workers. He put together the "standouts", people standing with my political signs, on his own. Each one was a success.

The September primary was coming fast. Voters could vote for four people. By now, I knew that I would finish sixth, behind the four incumbents and Buonomo. I worried that John would be hurt terribly. He had become so dedicated to the campaign. He really wanted me to do well. His loyalty never wavered for a moment. All this time, working with lots of people and in crowds.

I did finish sixth. He didn't say very much. As much for John as anything, I determined that we would not be embarrassed in the final election. We kept on working.

Did I mention that John never missed a single night of the Thursday Night Dinner Program for people with AIDS and HIV that we had founded and that we ran? Those nights were not quite as peaceful. We almost killed each other in the kitchen on more than one occasion. He had his night each month to do the work and yours truly would not let him do it his way. I got thrown out of the kitchen on more than one occasion. He got the meal out.

I hate to think how we must have sounded to the rest of the volunteers.

Election night came. We both knew the results well in advance. This time we had talked about what would happen. But we dreamed until the first results came in and then it was over. We were not embarrassed. Publicover got 34% of the vote, the same as in the primary. That was a good show.

I wish that I could tell you if I ever thanked John for all the work and the unending loyalty. I hope that I may have, but I took an awful lot for granted. He made that race possible.

We talked very little about the loss, if at all. I did say that I would think about running again in two years if we were healthy and if there was an opening on the Board.

My biggest concern was still that John must have been so badly hurt by my losing. Yet I never broached the subject with him. I did not want to bring up the subject once the race was over. I was in such fear of the mental anguish it might bring him at a time when he wasn't feeling very well.

Less than five months after the election, I was writing John's eulogy.

Not quite two months after John died, I told his friend and therapist, Lois, how concerned I was about his feelings when we lost. John had told Lois that she could repeat anything he had said to me.

John was worried more about how much the loss hurt me.

I should have known.

Someday, Thanks

Once in a while someone very special comes along. He may stay for a day or a week, or perhaps even a few months. You walk with him, talk with him, laugh with him. So few words, so many thoughts. You get nervous when he doesn't call, then the phone rings and you feel good again.

Happy is a feeling you seldom truly feel for very long. You can make yourself miserable. When he's not around, you wonder if he's going to tell you goodbye. You're with him and the same thought creeps into your mind every now and then. He says, "I like you, too," and your heart feels good.

You can call it love, or like, or friendship. He may leave you tomorrow and you'll feel like you've lost someone who can't be replaced. It's the end of the world. But deep inside, you know better. You'll recover, you always do. Those tears will dry.

So, tomorrow, if you see him, say "Thanks." Perhaps you'll continue together; maybe not. Call it like, call it love. Let it last as long as you both want it to. Someday, you'll remember these good times, whether you're together or apart.

Someday you'll remember, and you'll smile.

Please, Mister, Don't Play That Song

It probably played the night I met you.
You got angry when I played that jukebox
"I Don't Need You" was the song
It was Kenny Rogers and somebody else
The country stations were playing this one
And so were the local ones
Not long after we met.
I think you actually got angry
Each time that I said that was our song.
I never could sink into your head
Back then
The real meaning of the words.
They sang
"I Don't Need You"
Or the sun, or the air, or life.
For so long you did not get past the title.
It took a long time for you
To understand
About why I adopted that song
As one of ours.
It was so hard for me to say
I love you
Sometimes I had trouble telling myself.
Their music said it for me
And I knew
And you knew
Just how much I always needed
Your love.

January 1975

Alone—watching the late movie
Wondering what it would be like to have someone near
To touch—feel—to love—to care
I imagine him sitting with me
I look into his eyes—and he into mine
We feel something wonderful—something deep
I take his hand—he squeezes mine
A thrill goes through me
We're so close—like one
But I still sit alone—hoping—wishing
Praying that someday there will be someone here
for a long, long time.

Notes from the Seldom Kept CVS 3" x 5" Memo Book

<u>July 86</u>

Eating alone at the Grand Central Cafe in Provincetown. That's a first. I miss John and yet I can feel that I can go on OK. There's just an empty feeling.

I can afford to come here whenever I want to now—but do I really want to do it without my love or friends? I keep saying that I need 'self time.' Now that I have it, what will I do?

Things are not easy right now. Dad sick. John gone. No help at the paper. I don't feel helpless or hopeless. I've been through it before.

I wonder if someone like Lois could help me to find out what I'm not happy with in my life..

I don't expect John to come back...I would not say no if he did...I love him...even if we didn't come close to perfection. I can't hold any of this against him. Neither of us did as well as we could have. We both deserved better of each other.

I still love life and hope I'll be around for another 50 years. I just want to do more with my life. I know what I'd do if I had the courage.

<u>October 8, 1986</u>

Life can be so strange and change so fast. A week ago I got so upset setting John with Steve in P'town that I nearly (?) cried, yet it only took me a few hours to recover.

Then on Saturday, I met Jay. I don't know what clicked but something sure did. I knew in the first 5 minutes that something was happening here. For 2 weeks...2 months...Who knows. But my whole attitude has changed. I knew all along that there would be 'life after' the relationship but my time with Jay proved it. When he called Monday, I was so happy.

I said that my next relationship, if there is one, would be a smiling, happier one. It will be. I don't know what will happen with Jay but I sense something. I feel like I did when I met my first boyfriend...scared even to place that call.

November 28, 1986

Thanksgiving's over and it wasn't bad. I really hoped that John would call...maybe I should have tried to call him. I will in the next day or two. That Saturday night and my card may have shook him up.

It's sometimes almost scary to think that I may really be OK. I'm afraid that just as I get back on top, AIDS will knock me down. As time goes on, this will surely bother me less.

Life really does go on without John though I wish he was here. I'd like to really see if I could put all I say I have learned into reality to make a real relationship.

December 7, 1986

I'm not sure now if I'll go to Florida or to the Keys or not. I can't think of anywhere better.

I am really surprised that John has not been in contact for a month.

I cannot help but wonder if that night shook him up badly and he decided to have nothing to do with me. I am seriously considering going to P'town; not to confront but to see what happens. It could shake me up but I have virtually nothing to lose.

December 20, 1986

Tomorrow is the party and I look forward to it. I hope John comes to the party and on Christmas. It would truly make my holiday.

I'm looking forward to 1987 as a year where I'm me again. I don't know what will happen in my love life; not much I suspect but I'll manage whatever the future brings. Happy Holidays!

December 22, 1986

The party's over. It was a good party yet I feel like something was missing. There's that phone again. There were so few 'oldsters' there from the earlier days. Yet most of those that counted were there. Larry, Tim, Michael, Bill & Bill, Joe C. I guess that I should feel better. This still feels like an empty Christmas.

I tried to keep busy but how long can I do that. I want much if John shows up for Christmas but I know that I must expect very little.

Again this year, I was sorely disappointed with Sunday church services. There is no Christmas 'joy' in service. No real life.

You just can't keep 'em full. I got 3 more notices in 2 days from tenants.

December 26, 1986

It is the day after Christmas...wonderful Christmas. I thought I might spend most of the Eve and day alone but I didn't. As I hoped and yes, even believed, John was here with me. He was the John I always knew and loved. It was as if he had never left. Yet it was not; for if he had never gone, I could not appreciate how I felt and how I miss him and should have appreciated him so much more.

John seemed like he really cared. "I still love you!" That is not the first time he has said that and I hope not the last.

Will he return? I can't tell. I believe that he is thinking about it and is not sure what to do. How can I blame him? He wonders how much would change, if we would fall into the same old rut.

I don't know either but how I would like to try. One day, when the time is right, I will ask again for him to come home. I can honestly say that I look forward to 1987. We shall see about so much in the upcoming year.

December 30, 1986

I spent last nite in P'town with John. I think that he is going to come home after the winter. I cannot explain how much that scares me. It's exactly what I want yet now that it may happen, I'm petrified for both of us. If we work hard, and with God's help, we'll have a long, wonderful relationship. Amen.

January 2, 1987

John is coming home. It scares me but I can hardly wait!

Mr. Robert Publicover,
Publisher, The Somerville NEWS,.
Seven Davis Square
West Somerville, Mass.

Dear Bob:

I have your recent letter and am sorry to hear of your
illness.. Have hope! Keep on! I like to remember the words
one of the World's greatest doctor, Osler, had on a placard over
his operating room: "I wound. God heals."

Your case, I think, is best understood from the viewpoint
of what is known as the Instinc t Psychology of MacDougall.
MacDougall wrote many scientific books and was Professor of
Psychology at Cambridge (England), Harvard and Duke where he set
up the Department of Parapsycholgy. His viewpoint is not that of
the widespread psychology of today which is that of Watson -
Skinner "Behaviorism" and which has produced some of the social
attitudes you find exasperating.
MacDougall stressed that we are born with "instincts" - or "drives" -
of varying strengths and it is these that determine our lives rather
than acquired behavior.

With regard to the Bible. You should now be aware of what
many religious sects don't want you to know. Namely, that the
Bible comes to us through the minds of translators. For instance
there were forty-eight scholars and writers who, together, produced
the King James Version. What we have is THEIR interpretation of
the Latin,. Greek, Hebrew and Hebrew-dialect manuscripts.

But this is not the main point. You have demonstrated
exceptional ability in your work: Keep on! Who knows the future?
It would be my hope that you will find many years more of successful
accomplishment with reasonable health and persuasion.

Sincerely,

(Rev.) Elmer D.. Colcord

II Morrison Avenue
West Somerville, Mass.
May 8, 1922

You Loved Too Much

Those long nights are etched in my memory.
Your last four weeks
I cried, I wailed at times
When I realized your time was ebbing
The night after your nurse called
She was so worried.
The night after we all came and waited
At your bedside
Not knowing if you would leave us.
That night after, no one came but me, at midnight.
I was not ready for you to go.
I shut the door.
No one here would bother us.
Carefully,
I laid out the candles you loved
Lit them.
On the ghetto blaster you gave me on a whim
Your music played from your week in Godspell
I took out your small round crystal
Noting that I did not know for what you used it
But you would
Placed it gently in your hand and held it there.
Four bibles at home, yet
That night I could not find even one
So, here was the Methodist hymnal
Why did I have that?
I could not complete the 23rd psalm
Without many tears
I let them come
Forever and ever, Amen.
You stopped shaking.
Your fever went down.
Was that the night I climbed into your bed
And held you
To stop those shaking chills?
You knew
That I was not ready.
You were determined
Though you could not speak.

You stayed for three more weeks
You stayed for me.
I loved you even more.
I understand.
Your loyalty never wavered
You loved too much
Nay
Not so.
You loved your way
Until the end.

Short Takes—"You Were Always..."

I never could say "I love you" very well or easily. I did so often during those last few weeks in the hospital. I know that John heard me each time. Until the last few days, he would squeeze my hand to acknowledge when I spoke to him. It was the only communication we had.

So many times I have wondered why it was so hard for me to say those three words. But it was. The first time that I told John that I loved him, it shook me up so badly that I cried as I spoke. I asked him to be my lover, my partner, my longtime companion, that day.

I had gone out and purchased a 45 record of Willie Nelson's "You Were Always On My Mind." The record played in the background as I held his hand. (I'm getting off the point, of not telling him how I really felt...)

I was cleaning out drawers in the dining room, which he had started cleaning on his only four days home from the hospital. Way in back, whether carefully put there or not, was a card. The card looked immediately familiar...

"The years have really flown by
since we fell in love...
and they've brought me new reasons
to love you more and more.

You've been my lover, my friend,
my partner, and my pal.

You've been strong
when I needed you to lean on,
and you've been tender
when I need you
to listen and understand.

Even though
I don't always remember
to tell you how much
I appreciate you each day,
You're still the
one who makes my heart beat fast.

You're the one
I want to come home to forever—the one I'll always love."

There was a red rose at the bottom of the card and a simple:
"Love, Bob."

I know I gave it to him some time during our last six months or year together. I know that I don't have to worry anymore if I told him just how I felt.

Short Takes—Back to Work

I'm not exactly sure when it was that Betsy rushed back into the office, looking quite upset. It was shortly before John's first stay in the hospital.

She came in and said to me, "You'd better come out here. John is sitting on the stairs, crying."

I must have looked pretty surprised as I hurried out the door to see what was wrong. Betsy, with her usual understanding, headed right on down the stairs and out the door.

John was sitting on the marble landing, half way up the stairs.

Not knowing what was happening, I sat down beside John, who still had tears in his eyes. I put my arm around him without a word.

"I got this far and my legs hurt too much to go the rest of the way up the stairs." He barely got out the next sentence. "And then they hurt so much, I couldn't go down either." John began to cry again.

Lord, how I could feel his pain. The mental pain that he was suffering may have been worse than the physical. It was a crushing moment for John.

I told him that he would be OK. That this was just a muscle problem that he was going through because he had been working more than he should. Then we slowly made our way up the remaining stairs to the office. John sat quietly for a while. He was soon back to being himself and back to working...

The incident was supposedly soon forgotten.

I wonder, though, if that day ever left his mind. It remains so vividly with me.

There's Somebody In Here

Last night
I went out into the world
Expecting nothing
Another night out
Not especially a great mood
Sitting quietly at the bar
A shadow over me that won't quit.
About ready to call it a night,
Stayed when friends arrived
For the company.
It was an accident that I met him.
Closed the bar
Opened the night.
The fire is still in there.
I don't get much sleep
When someone's that close.
I dreamed that I'd taken home
Someone special.
When I woke up
He was there
Beside me.
Two people
Right place, right time.
My friends have heard the plaintive cry
I just want to be me, again.
I find myself
Somewhere hidden deeply away
On a night that was perfect
The future unknown
I found my smile
I found my heart
Me.

...and Out There...

That night
Perhaps
You and God got together
Talked it over
And gave me back me.
Did I feel you there?
Do I now?
Did you give me a slap on the head
As I slept with him
With that still jealous look?
Did I then hear a whisper?
Feel your smile?
"Go for it"
Thank you
I love you
Farewell, for now
From this side of the Earth.

New Travels

The last time; the only time
I remember tears on a plane
A very long time ago
On the way to Stephen's funeral
In this same city.
Lightning struck him down at 16
Faster than the plague
The same results.
I will miss you when I travel
(With whom will I hunt for airport capuccino?)
Those were our best times
(No one to share the shrimp bar)
The laughs, fights, fun, nights
(Do you really want to rent a Lincoln?)
Discovering new places
(Eat at the Velvet Turtle in Phoenix)
A melancholy feeling invades
Those spaces where the excitement used to be.
After I tested positive in '85 we set out
To visit each place of importance
One more time.
Somehow
We knew that time was growing short.
When we couldn't travel any longer
You sat in your hospital bed
Cruise books at your side
Off to Phoenix, Hawaii again,
Finally made it to Europe
Cruising on The Ecstasy
(Who shall we take this time?)
We dreamed.
In our hearts
We reached them all.

Mind/Body
(Stories for the Northern Lights Retreat)

1. 1974
I was walking down West Cedar Street
I felt 'heavy' with worry, my body tired
Only 50 cents to my name
I had to decide what to do with it.
Cookies or a lottery ticket...
At the corner of the street
I held the quarter in my hand
My body felt a surge
Tara?
"I will never be without money again."
My body felt sheer empowerment
For the first time in my life.

2. 1986
I left my house
Not happy
Drove my car to the bar
Determined to go out for Christmas Eve
My body felt alone
And my mind.
He had left me
Empty body
I walked into the bar
He was sitting there
Smile. Grin. Wow!
My mind/body soared.

3. 1992
3 am - Joan, R.N., angel, tapped on the door
I woke up
Mind/body half asleep
"Bob, you'd better come."
I slowly started to dress
My mind/body not in full motion
"Bob, hurry!"
My body, my mind woke up,
Snapped to attention
I got to his bedside
Held his hand tightly
"I'm here"
"I love you."
Body, mind unknown
John took his last breath.
My body had no feeling
Numb.
No emotions left.

"For Henry"

Dearest Friend,

You asked me for advice on dealing with Grief. I am no expert but I have 'learned' so much in the past 10 weeks, about life, other people, myself. The price paid for this life lesson is still too high.

The books will tell you that everyone's Grief is different. I don't know, I only have my own, but I suspect that they are right. Read the books. They are a comfort. They do make you realize that you are not alone in your feelings. I especially recommend "How to Survive the Loss of A Loved One" and "Life After Loss." There were five different Grief books that kept me company on some of those dark nights. The two mentioned were great, two were awful, and the other one was o.k. "Loved One" has a companion workbook...it helped me get my feelings together. I have gone back and read the book and the workbook on several occasions.

Make sure you eat. The desire won't be there for a while. Eat a lot of little meals. Get some Carnation Instant Breakfast and keep some fruit in the house. Get on the phone and find friends who will have lunch and dinner with you. If you are going to eat out alone, bring a book or a magazine.

Use the phone when times get especially tough. Ask several friends when it's o.k. to call them. You'll be surprised how many will say there are no limits if you're in trouble. Don't hesitate to call them. Call three people in a row and talk...it helps.

Talk, that's good advice. Don't hold it in. Talk about your loss to anyone who will listen but especially to your friends. That's what friendship is all about. People may not understand your Grief, but your friends will still listen. They really do want to help.

Have you wailed yet? Not cried...wailed. If you have, then you know exactly what I mean. I did on occasion for weeks, even before John died. It is natural. Others in my support group assured me of that. It is terrible at the time. Wailing leaves you physically, mentally weak and even frightened, but it will pass. It is cleansing. You will feel just a bit better after.

I don't know when the crying will stop...two months or ten years. Folks assure me that everyone is quite different. One lady told me her husband had died 21 years ago and that she could still sit down and have a good cry. When you feel like crying, do it. Don't hold it in. You're just human. Keeping your emotions to yourself isn't the answer to getting through this period of Hell.

Don't be afraid to talk to the doctor about taking something to keep you a little more natural for a while. I am petrified of 'tranquilizers' but I got a prescription. It bothered me every time that I had to take one. They simply brought me back to being myself for awhile. I cut back from 2 a day to 1 a day to 2 halves a day and, after two months, I'm hardly touching them. They did what they were made to do and I'm glad that I decided to take them.

If you have faith in the Guy Upstairs, pray. Pray a lot. I asked Him on numerous occasions for strength to get through; He helped. I went to church more over the period when John was so sick then ever before. People knew what was going on and they cared.

Write. Write your feelings down. It will help get them out in the open. Try keeping a journal each day. Write to friends. Write poetry. Write anything that will put exactly how you feel on paper. If those miserable thoughts of Grief and Loneliness are on paper, they may not be as strong in your head, your heart, your soul.

As long as you let yourself rely on others, you are going to find again and again that people come through. People you don't expect will reach out to help. Some that you may think will be there, won't be. Accept that fact. It's easier than feeling hurt.

Keep busy. Find something to do. Visit friends. Go to meetings. Join a Grief support group. Read. Get out with friends. Do anything to keep busy. Don't sit home and feel bad for yourself. Plenty of feeling bad will come without your assistance.

You will be grumpy, temperamental. People around you will just have to understand that fact. You probably will have the 'dropsies' for awhile. I swear that I broke half my tea cups in a month.

Your mind won't be working very well. Grief takes up so much of the room in there. You may find it hard to get your act together at home or at work. You'll confuse easily. It will pass. Take a break when your mind starts swirling too fast.

It sounds corny but I believe that the sun is your friend. Get out in it. A sunny day feels better and so will you.

Don't make any major decisions for a while. Put off every possible major decision that you can for at least two months, and longer if you can. Your mind isn't working normally, and you don't want to do something that you will regret later. You'll know when you're ready to decide.

Do something for someone else. It will make you feel better to reach out and know that you have helped.

Stick to your regular routine as much as you can. You are still you, and you're going to have to be for a long time to come.

I've read five books on Grief. If I got two good pieces of advice from each book, it was worth reading. You have to do all this in your own way. This letter won't tell you everything about getting through. I hope that I've helped.

As tough as this terrible loss is to you, you will get through it. Your loved one would want that. Tell yourself that often. You know it is simply the truth. There were times when I got so angry at my Grief because I knew that John would never want me to feel this bad.

Repeat after me:

I will survive.

Keep repeating that fact.

It is a fact.

You will survive.

God bless.

Life Spiral

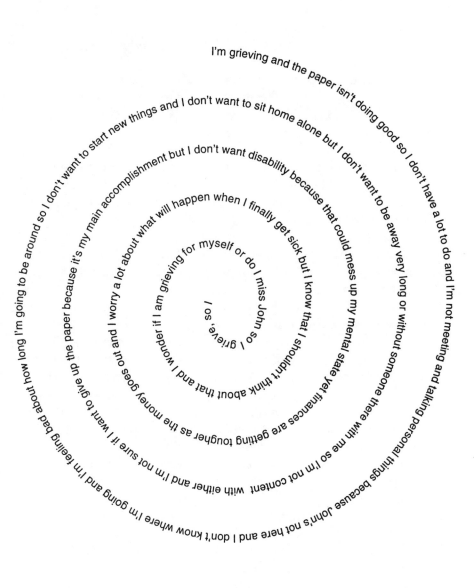

I'm grieving and the paper isn't doing good so I don't have a lot to do and I'm not meeting and talking personal things because John's not here and I don't know where I'm going and I'm feeling bad about how long I'm going to be around so I don't want to start new things and I don't want to sit home alone but I don't want to be away very long or without someone there with me so I'm not content with either and I'm not sure if I want to give up the paper because it's my main accomplishment but I don't want disability because that could mess up my mental state yet finances are getting tougher as the money goes out and I worry a lot about what will happen when I finally get sick but I know that I shouldn't think about that and I wonder if I am grieving for myself or do I miss John so I grieve, so I

Bluntly Speaking: Friends
(*The Somerville News*, June, 1985)

Do you tend to take your friends for granted? How often do you say "Thanks" when a friend lends a helping hand? When a good friend passes away, have you thought, "I wish I'd told him/her how much that person really meant to me."

I've been thinking about writing a column about Friendship for quite a while, yet I've never been sure where to begin or what to write. There is so much intangible about real Friendship and so many different versions of what Friendship really means.

I haven't seen my Best Friend, Larry, more than 4 times in the past three years. Yet, I know that if I picked up the phone and told him that I needed help, he'd be here in an hour, no matter what the time of day. I would do the same for him. Neither of us would ask any questions. That's Friendship.

When Dennis got out of jail after 7 years, I was one of the first people that he visited. I hoped that he had changed, that he was honest. A month later he borrowed a large sum of money, $500. I lent it to him in hopes that he had learned something about real Friendship. I have not seen Dennis since. He put the price of Friendship at $35 per year for the 14 years that we knew each other.

Dave Stryker was 62 years young when I first visited Xanadu Graphics. I wanted to inquire about the price of typesetting the newspaper which I wanted to start. Dave had owned his own newspaper and was glad to sit down many times over the next 5 years and give me advice. In the very beginning, he never asked for money up front from my new venture. Dave felt he could trust me. We became good friends over that short 5 years before he passed away, two weeks ago. Dave ended up not working for me but with me at *The Somerville News*. A friend that will be missed.

There are so many little things that friends do, little things that change your life. Tom August hired me when he was Mayor to work at City Hall, and my life has been uphill ever since. Fifteen years ago, a lawyer heard that I was not going back to college because I didn't have the tuition for another semester. Seems I had spent so much time working on a political campaign that I hadn't saved any money. That lawyer sat down and wrote me a check for $159 to cover tuition.

I know many people that are in 'love' and have been married for years yet they are still not Friends, they are more like a working business. They are working at raising a family. Yet I know others whose love has become a Friendship and that so often can mean much more. You start as 'lovers' but you become Friends. The flame doesn't die, it glows brighter.

You don't have to see a Friend at all for that Friendship to continue for many years. One may get a hundred Christmas cards this year, but the one from Jeanne in Chicago whom you haven't seen for a dozen years will mean more than most.

There can never be a price put on Friendship. Peter used to knock on the window of the bakery and call me in for a cup of 25 cent coffee, way back when. He knew that I was so broke that I could not afford that coffee. Before he passed away a few months ago, I tried to thank him. He wouldn't hear of it, not a word.

Maybe I was wrong. Real Friendship doesn't need to be spoken of or thanked for. Real Friendship is there; it doesn't need a single word. You just know it.

Bluntly Speaking: "Living" with HIV
(*The Somerville News,* June 24, 1992)

I wrote the article that follows in early January for publications at a later time. I put it on my partner's desk for his opinion. I honestly don't know if John ever read it. He entered Somerville Hospital that week.

I considered editing this column but decided it should stand as written. There is a time when a person has to make a decision. I have written in our city for 24 years. I have always told you exactly what is going on in my mind There is no reason to change now. I hope to keep writing for you and to you for a long time.

I have lived with HIV infection for seven years. I suspect that the reality is several years longer. These years have not always been easy, but my early knowledge of the infection has to be described as a blessing in disguise.

During these years, I have been lucky. I have never had an "opportunistic infection." Until this month, my T-cell count has been high enough that I could almost put the idea of the infection, the idea that it will be fatal one day, aside.

Many HIV-infected people do not discover that they have the infection until it is too late. People hide their heads in the sand, refusing to go for 'the test' despite being in a high risk group. One day they wake up too sick to live their lives as they could have. That will never be my regret.

Some people leave their jobs to discover the world out there while they still can. Some are luckier than others. Magic Johnson may indeed be a hero for telling the world, but I have to believe that having millions of dollars makes it easier to go public. It also makes it a heck of a lot easier to retire. Some of us have to go one making a living to survive without going on the public dole. Some of us are lucky enough to be able to continue working.

One of the great discoveries of my life after testing positive in 1985 for the virus was that I really did not want to make major changes. I liked what I was doing. Running a local newspaper and having a voice in the community is a wonderful job...even in this economy.

The early shock of infection wore off quicker than I thought it would. Probably, in part, because I knew back then that I had 5-10 good years ahead of me. The time flew, and recently I began to wake up to the fact that my longest years could well be behind me. It was not a though to be dwelled upon.

My involvement in the community has always given me a sense of accomplishment. As the founder (before my test) of the local AIDS Response Committee, I feel like I have been doing something that is right.

A few weeks after my positive test, the new minister of my church called to tell me that I was "needed" on the Board of Trustees. He was looking for new blood. He was looking for a big mouth who would speak out. He got it. I served two of these three years as President of the Board and then moved over as Chairman of the Pastor/Parish Relations Committee of the church.

The Committee For A Response to AIDS, of which my partner was co-chairman, continued its work. Slowly, we began to not feel like "voices in the wind" any longer. The folks that we kept telling that they would one day be affected by the AIDS virus have been coming back to tell us that we were right. We hear it every day. We never say "I told you so." We try to help.

When my partner, John, finally took the test nearly three years ago, we got our second shock. He not only tested positive, but had a T-cell count of 86. He immediately went on AZT. Its usefulness has since run out, and now he takes DDI, but for three years, he did not have an opportunistic infection. Despite being a much different type of personality than I am, he went on. He helped on the Committee. He knew that his time was limited, but didn't wallow in that fact.

Last year, I chose to run for city-wide office. I did so because I was not happy with some city officials. I did so because I realized that I might not have another opportunity while in good health. I lost with 34% of the vote. It was one of the richest and most rewarding experiences of my life.

We have always rented rooms in our home to make ends meet and pay the mortgage. It was a profitable idea, but these days and with this economy, the calls are few. We listed with the Boston AIDS Action Committee and have had several HIV-positive and PWAs (People With AIDS) live in our home.. It upsets me greatly to see people in far better shape than my partner sit in bed, watching TV all day every day. They could easily be out there doing something. I think that these are the guys that have inspired John, with his T-cell count down to 23, not to throw in that proverbial towel.

Our committee sponsors a Thursday Night Dinner Program each week for PWAs, HIV-infected people, and their friends. It functions as much more than a free meal. The dinners become a kind of internal support group. People talk about themselves, their medications, their politics. It amazes some of our volunteer cooks and servers when they listen to the talk and discover that those moaning the loudest about their health are sometimes in far better shape than the person clearing the table or the guy washing dishes in the kitchen. Some live with HIV. Some suffer.

Do I ramble? The key word in all of this essay in *"living."* It doesn't matter if you are living with HIV, living with cancer, living with poverty. You can live if you put your mind, your heart, your faith to work. I have seen homeless people who are not unhappy. I have watched people with no money give thousands of volunteer hours to charity. You can live with your trouble, your disease.

Our time is limited, so my partner and I go on about our lives, taking a little more time to smell the roses, a little more time to appreciate life; a little more time to help other folks.

We are not heroes. We simply appreciate the fact that we are still living, and intend to make the best of it.

"Living" with HIV is indeed possible.

* * *

John H. Carabineris, Jr., died of AIDS complications on March 24, 1992.

Short Takes—Sharyn's Visit

John had not been doing well for several weeks. He might have a few words to say on any given day but he was obviously failing. I fed him daily, a bite at a time, with Italian ices. That became our only real form of communication. He could still move his hands but with little control.

I could not decide whether or not to bring up our niece Sharyn, who was only 8 years old at the time, for a visit. It was not easy to know if it would be too traumatic for her to see her loved Uncle in this condition. I wondered what John would want. Would he prefer her to remember him as the healthy, fun, full of life man that he had been? He was certainly in good enough mind to know her if she came to the hospital. As always, his family left the decision to me. The decisions were never easy.

I spoke to Lois, John's friend and therapist. She told me that we would be amazed at a youngster's ability to understand and at what they could handle.

The next day, I called his sister and suggested that she should bring Sharyn. Nancy decided to bring our 2-year-old godson, Shawn Michael, also.

When I walked into his hospital room that night, Nancy, Sharyn, and Shawn Michael were already there with him. John had the first smile I had seen in quite a while. He was gripping a stuffed bunny with all his life. Sharyn talked to him and held his hand. That smile never left his face. You could sense a smile deep inside him. I wished only that he could talk to her. It must have been so frustrating for him.

Nancy and the two kids finally decided that it was time to leave. I sat beside John's bed knowing that I had made the right decision. He still held tightly to that bunny that Sharyn had brought with her.

He moved his lips trying to say something.

I leaned over as close as I could until his lips were right at my ear. I did not expect him to be able to speak but wanted to show him that I was trying to listen.

"That's what I really wanted, you know."

That was all he said. That was enough.

Dear Grief*

(*This letter and the next ones are exercise suggestions from "Life After Loss" by Bob Deits.)

January 22, 1992
9:20 p.m.

Dear Grief,

I can't say that I hate you like I did three months ago come Wednesday. I understand that you are a part of my life. You've been tough on me yet I've survived. Yes, I am a better person for your being around. I am stronger, I think. I certainly care more for those around me and appreciate them. I understand me a bit better.

I know you're still here. Your presence is felt often. Yet, you have cleansed me. There is a part of me more open, more ready to go on with the rest of my life.

Yes, I still miss John terribly. But I am more able every day to do what he wanted me to do; go on with my life. You have made me only more determined to live and live and live. I'm not going to give you the opportunity to visit my family and friends for a very long time.

Sincerely yours,

Bob

Dear Bob

June 23, 1992

9:25 p.m.

Dear Bob,

I have never told you that I was an easy one to endure or even get along with. You never really asked. I think you have avoided contact with me in the past. That makes the pain of losing John even worse.

I know that your life will never be the same; that you felt such pain and still have that emptiness. Think about it; would you rather not know me at all? Would you rather that someone you love die and that I just was not there?

You will be a better person for my visit. I'll probably never leave you entirely. You are already a more compassionate, caring person. You understand life—and death—a bit better.

You did not make a 'choice' to love, nor do you choose to grieve. You will find at some point that I am a cleansing process. Despite me or thanks to me, you will survive and more.

You know, as I do, that John wanted that for you. That's what my brother, Love, is all about. Rest assured that I can probably never bring you this much pain again in the future.

Sincerely yours,

Grief

Dear John

June 23, 1992
9:30 p.m.

Dear John,

I have to say good-bye to you. Our memories are forever and I will always treasure them. The 'Grief' book says I should buy fancy paper for your letter. Hell, no, we communicated on notebook paper for 10 1/2 years.

I miss you. I dearly wish that I had appreciated you more. I wish that I had loved you better and told you so much more often. I found that card I gave you which said it all. I was so relieved to remember that I had said all those things I wanted to say.

Despite our tough times, I loved you. You were a wonderful, caring man who matured so much over the years. You really became my partner in life and business and my best friend.

John, I'm sorry for the times I told you that you were no good, that you couldn't do anything. That was abusive and you did not deserve it. You were just you; and we both knew that I did often try to mold you into the image I wanted.

I hope you saw all of those who came to your wake and funeral. That sure would cure your insecurity. They came for you, John, not for me. People, so many of them, got to love you for ten years. And the cars from Danvers lined up to wait for you.

I will keep my promise to you to live as long as I can. I miss you so but I still love life; and there is so much more to do. I'm still thinking of the consignment store to help PWAs. Maybe it's not too late.

John, when I told you at your beside that I believed that we would meet again, I believed it. I don't know where that came from but it did. Maybe all the way from my soul. I still do. That's pretty amazing from me; you know that I don't believe in an after-life.

And now, I will, I must go on with my own life. I'm not just me, for you will always be in there. You made my life better. I know that you would say "Go for it." I will.

I love you. Farewell, for now.

Love,
Bob

So Long, I Love You

Back in 7th grade, most of us read the famous opening words to a great novel. "It was the best of times, it was the worst of times."

That is how I have felt about these past few days. A few months ago, after John had spent a week in the hospital with just the flu, we were being quite realistic and decided that we should make arrangements for both of us. We figured that our own Methodist church people would come and a batch of folks from the Baptist church, people from Danvers, the choir... He wondered if his entertainment friends would come and what about all those political people he had met over his years at the News and working in my campaign? Would anyone from Kiwanis or the Masons be there? How about the Mayors he knew, Capuano and Brune and August?

I assured him that they would surely all come. That Somerville people liked him. His face lit up and he said "I'm going to have quite a wake." I remember the kind of silly but satisfied look. He was quite proud of who might come to see him off. And you all came. My tears last night were not of sorrow but of pride. If any more of you had sent flowers, we wouldn't have been able to find John.

John Hedley Carabineris, Jr. came to my home to visit one night back in 1981. He never left. He was a great companion and good company. He began working for the Somerville News because he needed a job. He soon became indispensable. Each year, I had to give him a higher title, which he always snickered at. I finally ran out of titles and just named him Assistant Publisher.

When I introduced John as my partner, many folks were not sure just what I meant. Sometimes, neither was I.

John was a country boy. He loved his birthplace in Danvers, far from the turmoil of the big city. But he came to love Somerville and its people... He would never quite admit that he had become one of us crazy Somerville folks but the more people that he got to know here, the more he liked his home and the more people came to like John.

In 11 years John came to truly love this city and its people. He finally came to understand about Somerville. He loved delivering the News all over the city and greeting the people at places like Caradonna's and Todi's Subs every two weeks. He got to know many of them by name. He loved his dinners with the waitresses at the Mt. Vernon. He had so much fun kidding around with his fellow choir members.

The one place he had to go on his first day out of the hospital was for a cup of coffee at LaContesa to see everyone. He wasn't in any shape to do it and Dr. Bingham thought he was crazy. But it turned out to be his last trip to the bakery. No regrets.

John's courage after learning that he was HIV+ grew stronger every day. At first he was scared but he soon took a new spirit into his life. He helped to found the Thursday Night Dinner Program and AIDS Kitchen Kart. He worked at the dinners no matter how poorly he was feeling. He seldom complained except when it was to throw me out of the kitchen.

John would get so aggravated when he listened to Thursday Night Dinner Program diners "moaning and groaning." All of their T cell counts were higher than anyone's working in the kitchen. But they inspired him to work harder. The day after he got out of the hospital in January, he took a cab to the dinner. He was in such bad shape that I had to send him back home in a cab after a half hour. But he wanted to be there.

He spent three more days at home and that Sunday, went back into Somerville Hospital. And God how he loved those nurses. The nurses on 6B are angels who earned their wings with the wonderful way they treated John and me as his illness grew worse.

As his health worsened, he could seldom talk. He could barely move his hands but he tried to open every one of those cards from all of his friends. They came every day without fail. At the end, I read him every one.

He loved his family. The night I let his niece, Sharyn, in, he whispered, "That's what..." he was waiting for.

John liked people. He was a loner who learned just how great people could be. He would be so proud to see all of you who came to the wake yesterday and are here tonight. I'm sure he's up there right now, looking down at this long, music-filled service with that famous John sparkle in his eyes.

I have to share with you the night a little over two weeks ago. I walked into his room. He had not spoken more than a few words for over two weeks. I walked into his room and he waved and said, "Hi, how ya doing?" I was thrilled to hear his voice.

I never dreamed that we would talk for a solid hour. It was our little miracle and we both knew it. John's sister Nancy was there and we will treasure that hour for the rest of our lives. We even had him call his Mom. I would like to have seen the look in Grace's eyes when she realized it was Johnnie on the phone.

When John and I realized that we were both HIV+, we had long since founded the Committee For A Response to AIDS. We decided to let the world know a little at a time. We decided to reach out to our friends and to many others to let them know about the plague of AIDS. We decided to do our best to help people with HIV and to educate those who did not understand the disease.

At first, we were but "voices in the wind," but that changed over the past eight years. We kept telling people that they would see AIDS hit close to home. Over the years, so many have come to us to say that now they understand, as a friend, a neighbor, or relative was discovered to have the virus, or died.

John's last wish was to come home for his final days. When we asked for volunteers to help him, the phone rang off the hook. Our friends called and so did many people that we never met. When John came home last Monday, he knew he was where he wanted to be. We lit all those candles that he loved to have around and put on his own music from Godspell.

His eyes opened wide and we could see that old John Carabineris sparkle again for several minutes. John knew he was home.

When his time came to leave us, at 3 a.m., his night nurse from Somerville Hospital had volunteered her day off to be with him. She came and woke me and I spent his last few minutes, holding his hand.

John shed tears as he departed this life. He loved us all and he didn't want to leave us. But he left us something special, his love, his courage, his heroism in adversity.

John Hedley Carabineris, Jr., one man can make a difference in people's lives and you did.

So long—I love ya.

One More Time: Acknowledgements

Inspiration comes from many sources.

I sat down and wrote "Oh God, How I Love..." for myself on the day that I realized that my Lover was not going to get better. This book is a direct result of the inspiration that John Hedley Carabineris, Jr. provided.

Lois Levinsky, John's therapist, whom I started working with after his death, was the only person to whom I could think to send that piece. I continued to write after John's death, and Lois kept telling me that other people could be helped in their tough times by my writing. That thought makes it worthwhile.

Watching my best friend, Larry Doten, as he read my work each Friday when he visited, kept me going. I would always see a difference in him when he read these poems and stories.

Kathy, Joan and Rick took the time to read most of these works as I was still writing. Each of them encouraged me to continue. Each time that I left a piece for Betsy, a note would appear the next morning on my desk suggesting that it was better than the last one. Encouragement sure helps. (She liked it so much, she later typed and designed the book for me.)

David Penn urged me to self-publish and donated the use of his equipment and expertise. Those of us in the business are supposed to know how to do that, so I decided to take the shot. I never knew that Edgar Allen Poe and Mark Twain published many of their own works. Thanks, guys.

I want to thank several people whom I have never met. The authors of "How to Survive the Loss of a Love" are Melba Cosgrove, Ph.D., Harold H. Bloomfield, M.D. and Peter McWilliams. I purchased their book and workbook on the night after John's funeral. Their writing did wonders in helping me to keep my life together. The same can be said of Bob Deits, the author of "Life After Loss." The writings of these people inspired me to publish so that I might help others in their time of grief.

The inspiration for this work also came from the many friends who reached out during the worst weeks of my life. All the gang at the Thursday Night Dinner Program, many of the people at my church and those at Community Baptist, Fran, Danielle, Kathy and Tom at the Mt. Vernon, Rev. Larry French, Doug Petersen, Mike Markowski, Julie Druker, Deanna Kurlowicz, Tim Kozlowski, Clare and Toby, Rita, Sis, Nancy, Dr. Alex Bingham and a host of others.

I remember thinking that the red-neck Republican joke tellers at Kiwanis would never understand what I was going through. They were the very first ones to show up at John's wake.

The good really does come out in people when it counts.

Thanks, one more time, to all of you.

Carpe diem!

About The Author

Robert J. L. Publicover has been a resident of Somerville, MA, for all of his fortysomething years. He has published his award-winning independent, free newspaper *The Somerville News* for 12 years, and has written his column, "Bluntly Speaking," since 1969. Politically Bob has been accused by some of being conservative and by others of being too liberal. He is outspoken, energetic, optimistic, and boundlessly enthusiastic—all qualities that perhaps helped keep the HIV virus at bay for more than seven years.

Bob is also a man of courage. During his partner John's illness, he wrote in his newspaper column about a special trip they'd taken together, in a piece (included in this book) about doing things with those you love before it's too late. A pillar of the community who had always kept his personal life *very* personal, Bob proudly listed himself as "longtime companion" in John's obituary to all the area newspapers, announcing their relationship to all the world. In a later column in his own paper, after John's death, he publicly discussed his own HIV status, in an article about living life to the fullest (also included here).

Bob is passionately involved in his community. A man of deep faith, he is very active in his church and in numerous civic organizations, and he even made a run for the city office of Alderman-at-Large. He and his late partner, John, were also actively involved in organizing the Somerville Committee For A Response To AIDS, which later branched out to serve many surrounding communities. They organized a weekly dinner program for people with AIDS, a food cart collection program, and helped people with HIV and AIDS in numerous ways.

Even through the darkest days of John's illness and death, Bob managed somehow to carry on. In this volume he writes of his grief, his soul searching, and reflects on the many happy, special times spent with John, his life partner, his love.

This is not just a "gay book" or even an "AIDS book." It is a human book about the basic, deepest trials of life and faith, about love, loss, joy and sorrow.

My Unicorn Has Gone Away

For additional copies of *My Unicorn Has Gone Away*, simply complete and mail the order form below or call (617) 666-1848.

Also available from
Powder House Publishing

My Unicorn Has Gone Away
On two 90-minute cassette tapes read by the author $19.95

I Never Sang About Unicorns
The Music of John Hedley Carabineris, Jr.
On Cassette $12.95

Autographed copy of *My Unicorn Has Gone Away*
with a personal message from the author $24.00

- -

Please send me: _____ hardcover editions at $14.00 $ _____

_____ autographed editions at $24.00 $ _____

_____ Cassette sets at $19.95 $ _____

_____ *I Never Sang...* cassettes at $12.95 $ _____

~~~~~~~~~~~~~ *Add $3.00 per item for postage and handling* ~~~~~~~~~~~~~

_____ items at $3.00 $ _____

TOTAL $ _____

Bill my (circle one):   VISA   MasterCard   Discover

Credit Card # _____ Exp. Date _____

Name _____

Address _____

City _____ State _____ Zip _____

Telephone (____) _____

Make Checks Payable and Mail to:
Powder House Publishing, Box 137, Somerville, MA 02144